KENT AUTHORS TODAY

Some publications by the same editor:

New Hyperion (poetry and criticism), 1950

Literary, Debating and Dialect Societies of Great Britain, Ireland and France, *5-parts*, 1950–1953

A Selected Bibliography of Literature Relating to Nursery Rhyme Reform, 1952. Several reprints

Winifred Holtby Bibliography and Letters, 1955

John Gay and the Ballad Opera (with Frank Granville Barker), 1956

The Book of the Private Press (with Thomas Rae), 1958

John Masefield, O.M.—The Queen's Poet Laureate (a bibliography) with an essay by G. Wilson Knight, 1960.

Selected Letters of Winifred Holtby and Vera Brittain, 1920–1935 (with Vera Brittain), 1961. Academic Reprints new edition, 1970

Bibliography of Monaco, 1961. Second enlarged edition, 1968

Bibliography of Iran, with a memoir by Ardeshire Zahedi, 1964. Fifth enlarged edition, 1969

C. Day Lewis, Poet Laureate (a bibliography) (with Timothy d'Arch Smith)—preface by W. H. Auden, 1968

Lancashire Authors Today, 1971

Yorkshire Authors Today, 1972

Authors of Wales Today, 1972

Scottish Authors Today, 1972

Cheshire, Derbyshire and Staffordshire Authors Today, 1972

Berkshire, Hampshire and Wiltshire Authors Today, 1973

Devon, Dorset and Somerset Authors Today, 1973

Kent Authors Today, 1973

Sussex Authors Today, 1973

2.50

Kent Authors Today

BEING A CHECKLIST OF AUTHORS BORN IN
KENT TOGETHER WITH BRIEF PARTICULARS
OF AUTHORS BORN ELSEWHERE WHO ARE
CURRENTLY WORKING OR RESIDING IN KENT
. . . AN ASSEMBLAGE OF MORE THAN 530
AUTHORS TOGETHER WITH THEIR ADDRESSES
AND (WHERE APPLICABLE) THEIR PSEUDONYMS

Hon. General Editor
GEOFFREY HANDLEY-TAYLOR
Ph.D., F.R.S.L

EDDISON PRESS LTD.
Publishers of County Authors Today Series
LONDON SW1
1973

2 Greycoat Place, London SW1P 1SB
© 1973 Eddison Press Ltd.,

SBN 85649 011 3
Library of Congress Catalog Card No. 75–189268

Printed in Great Britain by Bristol Typesetting Co. Ltd.,
Barton Manor, St. Philips, Bristol

Contents

Preface

In the compilation of this eighth volume in the County Authors Today Series, as always, particular care has been taken to draw attention to the work of the local historian—that often neglected specialist who may rarely achieve recognition beyond the area he has treated. Examination of *Kent Authors Today* reveals a notable cross-section of writers specialising in the subjects of theology, horticulture, ornithology, art and architecture. Where we have been unable to establish the birthplace of an author, the general practice has been to include that author's entry in the section headed "Authors resident and/or working in Kent who were not born in the County". Where an author provides the address only of his literary agent or publisher *outside the county*, unless there is a qualifying footnote ("this author resides in Kent"), for the purpose of this publication, the author is regarded as non-resident in the county. Only rarely does an author request us to exclude his or her entry from the checklists in this series on the grounds that inclusion will create for him or her unwelcome invitations to lecture to local societies or write for local publications. In general, authors surely welcome local and county recognition. Thus this series is intended to serve both the author and the community.

In the present checklist, as in those previously published in the series, author migration tells its own story. This text assures us that few authors only manage to subsist entirely upon the proceeds of writing. As always, most authors have to follow other bread-winning occupations. It will be seen that the author's principal occupation, particularly if other than authorship, is stated when such information has been ascertained.

Specially introduced into these pages is a system of coding (where applicable—noted at the conclusion of each author entry). This service assists the reader to note at a glance in which other reference works an author's biographical note or other mention of his or her activities appear. Observations relating to this innovation will be found in the section headed *A "Key" to the 81 Reference Works Coded in this issue of the County Authors Today Series*. Acknowledgement is here made for the valuable aid many of these 81 listed publications have provided during the research preparatory to the completion of this county checklist.

For the purpose of easy reference this text has been divided into four sections—as detailed below. (Birthplaces are printed in bold type for rapid area identification purposes.)

(a) *Authors born in Kent who are still resident and/or working in the County.* In addition to their pseudonyms (where applicable) there are 43 authors listed.

(b) *Authors born in Kent who are Currently resident outside the County within other areas of the United Kingdom.* 184 authors are listed. In addition, pseudonyms (where applicable) are indicated and are the subject of cross-reference.

(c) *Authors born in Kent who are currently resident and/or working overseas.* 18 authors are included in this category with addresses in Australia, Canada, France, Ireland, Italy, Malta, Portugal, Republic of South Africa, and U.S.A.

(d) *Authors resident and/or working in Kent who were not born in the County.* 289 authors are included in this section.

From the information above it will be seen that of 245 authors born in Kent only 43 still reside there. Some 289 authors born elsewhere, however, compensate for the large exodus of native-born authors.

Although there are more than 530 authors listed in this text, the editor and his staff, in undertaking the initial research traced and contacted Kent authors in excess of this figure. From several authors confirming data was not received in time for publication. Two authors requested exclusion from this text. The editor, therefore, does not pretend that he has garnered into these pages brief notes upon all existing authors of Kent. It is inevitable that even taking into account the number of authors excluded (mentioned above) there are others still to be traced. In future years, when (perhaps) another survey of authors in the area treated is undertaken, more authors within the county will have emerged and/or will have been traced. Until that day arrives, however, it is hoped that *Kent Authors Today* will fill a useful gap.

Although every care has been taken in compilation, the editor and his colleagues offer, in advance, apologies for any oversight or occasional inconsistency. For the most part the editor has worked from data furnished by the authors. Where this information could not be cross-checked in other available reference works, the information has been accepted at face value.

In conclusion, the enormous help of librarians and their staffs in Kent in the preparation of this compilation is most gratefully acknowledged. Without such generous and experienced assistance *Kent Authors*

Today would be less rewarding to those who consult the County Authors Today Series.

2 Greycoat Place,
London S.W.1.
20 June 1973.

George Handley-Taylor.

Acknowledgements

In the preparation of *Kent Authors Today* the honorary general editor acknowledges with thanks the assistance of the authors themselves. He also tenders grateful thanks to the following persons and institutions for help or advice given at various stages during compilation:
Ashford Branch Library (Mrs. J. Tindall, F.L.A., Branch Librarian); (Bexleyheath) London Borough of Bexley Reference Library (V. Whibley, A.L.A., F.R.S.A., Reference Librarian); Bromley, London Borough of, Public Libraries (A. H. Watkins, F.L.A., Borough Librarian); Canterbury, Royal Museum and Public Library (F. Higenbottam, B.A., F.L.A., City Librarian); Chatham Public Libraries (I. G. R. Stacey, Borough Librarian); Dartford Public Libraries (Stanley Atkin, A.L.A., Borough Librarian); Dover Public Library (A. J. Ricketts, A.L.A., Borough Librarian); Folkestone Public Library, Museum and Art Gallery (K. C. Sussams, A.L.A., Borough Librarian and Curator); Gillingham Public Libraries, Central Library (Norman Tomlinson, F.L.A., Borough Librarian); The Gladstone Library of the National Liberal Club, London (G. W. Awdry, M.A., F.L.A., Librarian); Gravesend Public Libraries, Central Library (Walter T. W. Woods, F.L.A., Borough Librarian); Kent County Library (Maidstone) (Dean Harrison, M.A., F.L.A., County Librarian); Maidstone and District Chamber of Commerce (Ronald G. Piggott, F.A.C.C.A., Secretary); Maidstone Public Libraries, Central Library (Alfred Joyce, F.L.A., Borough Librarian); Maidstone Writers' Circle (Miss Ruth Spencer); Sevenoaks Central Library (G. H. Lawrence, F.L.A., Librarian); Sittingbourne and Milton Public Libraries (Kenneth Chatfield, F.L.A., Librarian), and (Tunbridge Wells) Royal Tunbridge Wells Public Library and Museum (R. G. Bird, F.L.A., Borough Librarian).
Reginald L. Arundale; Michael Ayres; Helen S. Beere; The Editor of *The Book Exchange*; J. Malcolm Dockeray, A.R.M.C.M., Robin Gregory, B.A.; Ernest Kay, D. Litt., F.R.S.A.; David Fara Proudlove, and John W. Woodward, O.S.J.

A "Key" to the 81 Reference Works Coded in this issue of the County Authors Today Series.

In the course of our inquiries authors are invited to furnish details of the titles of other reference texts in which their biographical notes, or mention of their activities, have appeared. The result of the inquiry produces useful (confirming) reference data, and some 81 books listed below have been the subject of coding. This number will be added to as further titles in the County Authors Today Series appear and as necessity may demand. By glancing at the numerals shown at the end of each author's entry, users of this series can check in which other reference works an author is listed. It will be appreciated by users of this exclusive coding feature that in some cases no coding figures appear. For the most part absence of a numeral (or numerals) denotes that the author is being recorded for the first time in a reference text catering for authors. One other exception applies when an author has failed to provide confirming data.

1 signifies *Who's Who*
2   ,,   *Who's Who in America*
3   ,,   *Who's Who in Canada*
4   ,,   *Who's Who in Australia*
5   ,,   *Who's Who in New Zealand*
6   ,,   *International Who's Who*
7   ,,   *Who's Who in Europe*
8   ,,   *The Author's and Writer's Who's Who*
9   ,,   *The Writers Directory*
10   ,,   *Contemporary Authors* (U.S.A.)
11   ,,   *International Who's Who in Poetry*
12   ,,   *Contemporary Poets of the English Language*
13   ,,   *Science Fiction and Fantasy Who's Who* (U.S.A.)
14   ,,   *Dictionary of International Biography*
15   ,,   *Crockford's Clerical Directory*
16   ,,   *Catholic Authors* (U.S.A.)
17   ,,   *World Who's Who in Commerce and Industry* (U.S.A.)
18   ,,   *Directory of Directors*
19   ,,   *Who's Who in Music*
20   ,,   *Blue Book*
21   ,,   *Catholic Who's Who* (U.S.A.)
22   ,,   *Who's Who in Art*
23   ,,   *Who's Who in Science in Europe*

Authors born in Kent who are still resident and/or working in the County

BAKER, T(homas) F(rancis), B.A., Editor of Victoria County History of Middlesex. **TUNBRIDGE WELLS,** Kent, 1935. Publications include: "The Island Race", "The Normans", "Medieval London", etc. Camden Lodge, 50 Hastings Road, Pembury, Kent. *8.*

BAKER WHITE, John, T.D., J.P., Journalist, Author and Research Worker. **WEST MALLING,** Kent, 12 August 1902. Author of "Red Russia Arms", "Gone for Good", "Soviet Spy System", "Nationalisation: Chaos or Cure", "Pattern for Conquest", "Sabotage is Suspected", "True Blue", etc. Street End Place, Street End, near Canterbury, Kent. *1, 8.*

BALDWIN, R(onald) A(rthur), Investigating Officer, Inland Revenue. **GILLINGHAM,** Kent, 2 June 1914. Author of books on local history. 36 Stuart Road, Gillingham, Kent.

BIRD, William Henry, Barrister-at-Law, F.C.I.S. **KENT,** 1882. Secretary, The Institute of Brewing, 1908–1951. Author of "A History of The Institute of Brewing, 1886–1951". Sturry, Canterbury, Kent. *8.*

BIRT, Catherine. **SMARDEN,** Kent, 1917. Publications include: Royal Sisters (Vol. 1.), "H.R.H. Princess Margaret", "Princess Margaret's 19th Birthday Book", "H.M. Queen Elizabeth", etc. 16 Royal Chase, Tunbridge Wells, Kent. *8.*

BOORMAN, H(enry) R(oy) Pratt, C.B.E., D.L., M.A., F.J.I., Newspaper Proprietor and Editor. **MAIDSTONE,** Kent, 21 September 1900. *Awarded Sir Edward Hardy Gold Medal, Association of Men of Kent and Kentish Men (1964). Lord of the Manors of Bilsington Inferior and Bilsington Superior; Member of Kent County Council (1933–1946); Mayor of Maidstone (1962–1963); President, Newspaper Society (1960–1961); President, Home and Southern Counties Newspaper Proprietors Federation (1968–1969); Member, Court of Assistants, Worshipful Company of Stationers and Newspaper Makers (since 1966); Editor and Proprietor, "Kent Messenger" (1928–1952); Chairman of "Kent Messenger" Group of Companies (since 1952).* Publications include: "Hell's Corner", "Kent—Our Glorious Heritage", "Kentish Pride", "Kent Churches", "Kent Inns", "Kent and the Cinque Ports", "Kent Messenger Centenary", "Pictures of Maidstone", "Recalling the Battle of Britain", "Kent—A Royal County", "Spirit of Kent, Lord Cornwallis", "Tonbridge Free Press Centenary", etc. St. Augustine's Priory, Bilsington, near Ashford, Kent. *1, 8, 30, 32.*

B   3

BRIGDEN, Susan Jane. **ROCHESTER,** Kent, 1938. Author of "Billy Bun", "Maria", etc. Dolphin House, Victoria Street, Rochester, Kent. *8.*

BUCKINGHAM, Christopher, B.A.(Hons. History) (Exeter), School Master **CANTERBURY,** Kent, 20 June 1937. *Founder of "Cantium" and Editor, 1969 (ex officio member of editorial board).* Publications include: "Lydden, a Parish History", "Catholic Dover", "Pages from a Nova Scotian Journal" (poems). Wellington House, Lydden, Kent.

BURTON, Ernest James, M.A.(London), F.R.S.A. **CRAYFORD,** Kent, 1908. Publications include: "Teaching English Through Self-Expression", "Drama in Schools", "Students Guide to World Theatre", "Students Guide to British Theatre", "Theatre Alive or Dead?" (editor), "The British Theatre, 1100–1900", "The Communication of Religious Experience", "A Faith of Your Own", etc. Roseries, Monks Horton, Sellindge, Ashford, Kent. *8.*

BUSHELL, Thomas A(lexander), M.C.I.T., Secretary of Trust Funds (Retired) and House Magazine Editor. **CHISLEHURST,** Kent, 17 March 1899. *Chairman of Historical and Literary Committee of the Association of Men of Kent and Kentish Men (The Kent County Society), also Vice-President.* Publications include: "Royal Mail", "Eight Bells", "Kent: Our County", "A Chronological History of Kent". 48 Green Way, Chislehurst, Kent BR7 6JF.

CAMPBELL, Judith *see* PARES, Marion Stapylton.

CLARK, Commander Victor (Cecil) (Froggatt), D.S.C. (and bar), Royal Navy (retired). **DOVER,** Kent, 24 May 1908. Publications include: "On the Wind of a Dream". Schooner Captain Scott, Plockton, Wester Ross; and c/o National Westminster Bank Limited, 143 High Street, Bromley, Kent. *8.*

CLIFFORD, Derek Plint, M.A.(Cantab.), Writer. **GILLINGHAM,** Kent, 1 September 1951. Publications include: "Mad Pelynt and the Bullet", "The Perracotts", "Geraniums", "Pelargoniums", "A History of Garden Design", "Watercolours of the Norwich School", "John Crome" (in collaboration with T. P. P. Clifford), "The Paintings of Philip de Laszlo", "Collecting English Water-Colours", etc. Hartlip Place, Sittingbourne, Kent. *8.*

4

COPELAND, H(enry) Rob, Dip. F.D., M.B.I.E., Funeral Director. **BECKENHAM,** Kent, 28 June 1902. Publications include: "From Village to Borough", "The Manor of Old Beckenham", "The Village of Old Beckenham", etc. 114 Bromley Road, Beckenham, Kent BR3 2NU.

CUMMING, Primrose (Amy), Writer of fiction for children. **MINSTER,** Isle of Thanet, Kent, 7 April 1915. Author of some twenty titles, including: "No Place for Ponies", "Flying Horseman", "Mystery Trek", "Foal of the Fjords", "Penny and Pegasus", etc. Wynberg, Sandhurst, Hawkhurst, Kent. *8, 10.*

DAVIES, Margaret *see* DUNNETT, (Lady) Margaret (Rosalind).

DUNNETT, (Lady) Margaret (Rosalind), Author of novels for children. **TUNBRIDGE WELLS,** Kent, 15 May 1909. (*pseud.* Margaret Davies (maiden name)) Author of "The People Next Door", "Has Anyone Seen Emmy?", "The Gypsy's Grand-Daughter", "Max a Million", etc. Basings Cottage, Cowden, Kent. *8.*

EAMES, G(eoffrey) L(eonard), LL.B.(London), F.C.I.S., Company Secretary. **BROMLEY,** Kent, 4 March 1924. Author of "A History of Bromley Hockey Club, 1888–1963", "Bromley Cricket Club, 1820–1970". 23 Aldermary Road, Bromley, Kent.

EDWARDS, Enid, A.R.C.A. Teacher and Lecturer in Hand and Machine Embroidery. **LAMBERHURST,** Kent, 1914. Author of "Decorative Soft Toymaking". 40 Gerrard Avenue, Rochester, Kent. *8.*

GALVIN, Ronald Albert William, B.Sc.(Eng.), Lecturer. **DOVER,** Kent, 10 July 1926. Publications (in conjunction with J. O. Paddock): "Electrical Installation Technology and Practice", "Electrical Installation Science", "Electrical Principles for Installation and Craft Studies". 2 Farthingloe Road, Dover, Kent.

HARRISON, David L(akin), M.A., M.B., B.Ch., Ph.D.(Cantab.), Medical Practitioner. **SEVENOAKS,** Kent, 1 October 1926. *Awarded Bloomer Medal, Linnean Society of London (1966).* Author of "Footsteps in the Sand", "The Mammals of Arabia" (3 volumes), etc. The Harrison Zoological Museum, Bowerwood House, St. Botolph's Road, Sevenoaks, Kent. *8, 24.*

5

HARRISON, Jeffery G(raham), O.B.E., M.A.(Cantab.), M.B., B.Chir. (Cantab.), M.R.C.S., L.R.C.P., D.R.C.O.G., F.Z.S.(Sci.), F.L.S., M.B.O.U., Doctor of Medicine. **SEVENOAKS,** Kent, 28 July 1922. Editor, The Annual Reports of the Wildfowlers' Association of Great Britain and Ireland; Editor, Bulletin of the British Ornithologists' Club (1952–1962); Editor, The New Wildfowler; Editor, The New Wildfowler in the 1970's. Author of "The Birds of Malvern", "Estuary Saga", "Pastures New", "A Wealth of Wildfowl", etc. Merriewood, St. Botolph's Road, Sevenoaks, Kent. *8.*

HAYNES, Alfred Henry, Local Government Officer (retired). **DEAL,** Kent, 29 September 1910. Author of "Practitioner's Handbook to the Social Services", "The Boy Who Made Time Stand Still", "The Story behind the Stamp", "Some Stamps and their Stories", "This is Dover", "The Dagenham Girl Pipers", "The Story of Bowls", etc. 187 The Gateway, Marine Parade, Dover, Kent.

HAYNES, Edward George Ambrose, Local Government Officer (retired). **WALMER,** Kent, 1906. Author of "Heroic Messenger", "Three Victorious Girls", "Return of the Witch Doctor", "Helpful Penny", "Inquisitive Penny", "The Treasure of the Heidel Mountain", "The Daring Three", "Hans Gretel and Samelli", "David's Quest", "The Mystery of Boxling Woods", "Alpine Fugitives", "Greta's Dream", "Greta's Decision", "Spanish Galleon", "Peter's Adventurous Holiday", "Peter's Return", "Tony Stands Firm", "The Mystery of Portrock", "The Stowaway's Secret", "Holiday with Aunt Jessica", "The Mysterious Skipper Fenton", "Meet the Gunthers", "Pamela's Ambition", "Adventure on Purseyness"; also The Good Shepherd Series, etc. 10 White Cliff Way, Folkestone, Kent. *8.*

HIGHAM, Roger (Stephen). **DARTFORD,** Kent, 23 June 1935. Author of "Island Road to Africa", "Provencal Sunshine", "Road to the Pyrenees", etc. 39 High Street, Sturry, Canterbury, Kent. *8, 10.*

HOBO DIARIST *see* SANDERS, Frederick W(illiam) T(homas).

LADYMAN, Phyllis, Artist. **BROMLEY,** Kent. Publications include: "About a Motor Car", "Things About the House", "About Flowering Plants", "About Farm Machines", "Inside the Earth", etc. 10 Clarence Place, Gravesend, Kent. *8.*

6

LAKEMAN, Enid, BSc.(London), A.R.I.C., Director, Electoral Reform Society. **HADLOW,** Kent, 28 November 1903. Author of "When Labour Fails", "Voting in Democracies" (with James D. Lambert), "How Democracies Vote", etc. 37 Culverden Avenue, Tunbridge Wells, Kent. *8, 9.*

LONGRIGG, Brigadier Stephen H(emsley), O.B.E., M.A., D.Litt.(Oxon.), Civil Servant (Iraq) and Oil Company Executive. **SEVENOAKS,** Kent, 7 August 1893. *Awarded Lawrence of Arabia Medal (1962), Sir Richard Burton Memorial Medal (1970). Governor of Highgate School (1946–1965), Chairman (1955–1965).* Publications include: "Four Centuries of Modern Iraq", "Short History of Eritrea", "Iraq, 1900 to 1950", "Oil in the Middle East", "Syria and Lebanon under French Mandate", "Iraq" (in collaboration), "The Middle East, a Social Geography", etc. 58 Chancellor House, Tunbridge Wells, Kent. *1, 6, 8, 9, 30.*

MARSH, Ronald, F.L.A., Librarian. **BROADSTAIRS,** Kent, 7 August 1914. Publications include: "Family Jigsaw" (play), "Irene" (novel), "Your brother still" (novel), "The Quarry" (novel), "The Conservancy of the River Medway, 1881–1969". Central Library, Northgate, Rochester, Kent. *8, 9.*

NEAME, Alan John, M.A.(Oxon.), Editor and Religious Historian. **FAVERSHAM,** Kent, 1924. *Literary Editor of the Jerusalem Bible.* Publications include: "Adventures of Maud Noakes", "Exploration Diaries of H. M. Stanley", "Maud Noakes, Guerrilla", "The Happening at Lourdes", "The Psalms", etc. Fisher Street, Sheldwich, near Faversham, Kent. *8, 9.*

NEAME, Lt.-Gen. Sir Philip, V.C., K.B.E., C.B., D.S.O., D.L., Army Officer. **FAVERSHAM,** Kent, 12 December 1888. *President, Institution of Royal Engineers (1954–1957), Vice-President, National Rifle Association, President, North London Rifle Club,* etc. Author of "German Strategy in the Great War", "Playing with Strife: The Autobiography of a Soldier". The Kintle, Selling Court, Faversham, Kent. *1, 6, 8,*

NEWMAN, Leonard Hugh, F.R.E.S., Managing Director of Butterfly Farm. **BEXLEY,** Kent, 1909. Author of "Butterfly Farmer", "Transformations of Butterflies and Moths", "Butterfly Haunts", "British

Moths in their Haunts", "Looking at Butterflies", "Nature Parliament" (with Peter Scott and James Fisher), "Observer's Book of Insects" (with E. F. Linssen), etc. Betsoms, Westerham, Kent. *8.*

PADDOCK, J(ames) O(wen), F.I.E.E., Senior Lecturer. **DOVER,** Kent, 12 September 1927. Publications (in collaboration) include: "Electrical Installation Technology and Practice", "Electrical Installation Science", "Electrical Principles for Installation and Craft Studies". 43 Coxhill Gardens, Dover, Kent.

PARES, Marion Stapylton, Writer. **WEST FARLEIGH,** Kent, 1914. (*pseud.* Judith Campbell) Author of "Family Pony", "The Queen Rides", "Horses in the Sun", "Police Horses", "Pony Events", "World of Horses", "Horses and Ponies", "World of Ponies", "Anne —Portrait of a Princess", etc. Studfall Ridge, Lympne Hill, Hythe, Kent. *8, 9.*

PLANT, Jack. **FOLKESTONE,** Kent, 1926. Author of "Moppy's Great Adventure", "Let's Act It", "The Discovery of Plays" (Books 1 and 2, with John Anderson), "Spy Trail to Danger", "The League of the Purple Dagger", etc. 39 Alexandra Street, Folkestone, Kent. *8.*

PORTEOUS, L(eonard) G(odfrey) H(arold), Civil Servant. **DARTFORD,** Kent, 6 November 1918. *Hon. Editor, "Newsletter", Dartford Historical and Antiquarian Society (since 1964).* Author of published script "A Church, a Town", and of a Guide-book to Dartford Parish Church. 1 St. Saviour's Avenue, Dartford, Kent DA1 1RV.

PROUDFOOT, W(illiam) Frank, M.A.(Cantab.). **SIDCUP,** Kent, 27 November, 1909. Author of "Fawkham: The Story of a Kentish Village". Pennis House, Fawkham, Kent.

RAVEN, D(avid) S(ebastian), M.A., B.Litt.(Oxon.), University Teacher and Professor of Classics. **BROADSTAIRS,** Kent, 26 August 1933. Publications include: "Greek Metre", "Latin Metre", etc. East Cliff House, Broadstairs, Kent. *8.*

REID, P(ercy) G(ladwell), Journalist. **STROOD,** Kent, 19 September 1906. *President, National Union of Journalists (1961–1962) and*

Honorary Member since 1966. Publications include: "Churchill: Townsman of Westerham", "Westerham Amateur Dramatic Society: A Short History". 12 Westways, Westerham, Kent.

SANDERS, Frederick W(illiam) T(homas), engaged in Salvage, Ship-building, etc. **PLUCKLEY THORNE,** Pluckley, near Ashford, Kent, 9 August 1908. (*pseuds.* Wealden Wanderer, Hobo Diarist). Publications include: "Kentish Wealden Dialect", "Kent Weald Church-yards", "Natural History of Mundy Bois", "The Dialect of Kent", "Psychical Research in Haunted Kent", "Pluckley was my Play-ground", "A Business History of Chatham High Street, 1838 to 1961", "The Chatham Dockyard Diary", "Lawrence of Arabia", etc. 42 Sydney Road, Chatham, Kent.

SARGENT, Rev. Laurens Christopher, B.A., Clergyman. **NONING-TON,** Kent, 1893. Author of "Moenia Romae", "Consider the Birds", "Ulla-Britt and the Birds", "Letters in the Sand", etc. Parsoncote, Nonington, near Dover, Kent.   *8.*

SHAW, Otto Leslie, Ph.D., J.P., Psychologist. **BEXLEY,** Kent, 21 February 1908. *Chairman, Kent Magistrates Association; Chairman of a Juvenile Court; Chairman, Maidstone Labour Party; Fellow, Bibliographical Society; Fellow Chemical Society.* Author of " Mal-adjusted Boys", "Youth in Crisis", "Prisons of the Mind", etc. East Sutton, near Maidstone, Kent.

SPEAIGHT, Robert (William), C.B.E., M.A.(Oxon.), F.R.S.L., Author. **ST. MARGARET'S BAY,** Kent, 14 January 1904. *Appointed Officer of the Legion of Honour (France), 1969. Member of Council, The Royal Society of Literature.* Publications include: "Hilaire Belloc", "Eric Gill", "Teilhard de Chardin", "The Property Basket", etc. Campion House, Benenden, Kent.   *1, 7, 8, 9.*

WATERFIELD, Gordon, O.B.E., M.A.(Oxon.), Journalist, Author, and Broadcaster. **CANTERBURY,** Kent, 24 May 1903. Publications in-clude: "Lucie Duff Gordon", "What Happened to France", "Layard of Nineveh", "Sultans of Aden", etc. 1 Westfield House, Tenterden, Kent.   *8.*

WEALDEN WANDERER *see* SANDERS, Frederick W(illiam) T(homas).

9

WILSON, J(ohn) Greenwood, O.St.J., M.D.(London), F.R.C.P.(London), D.P.H.(London), F.K.C., Hon.F.R.S.H., Hon.F.A.P.H.A., Medical Consultant (retired). **CHARLTON,** Kent, 27 July 1897. Author of "Public Health Law in Question and Answer", etc. Flat 2, 10 Beckenham Grove, Bromley, Kent BR2 0JU. *1, 8, 9.*

Authors born in Kent who are currently resident outside the County within other areas of the United Kingdom

ALEXANDER, Boyd, B.A.(Oxon.), Dip. in Theology(Oxon.), Author, Lecturer and Researcher. **CRANBROOK,** Kent, 4 November 1913. Publications include: "Beckford's Journal in Portugal and Spain" (Ed.); "Life at Fonthill, 1807–1822, from the Correspondence of William Beckford"; "England's Wealthiest Son: a Study of William Beckford"; "Beckford's Recollections of an Excursion to the Monasteries" (Ed.), etc. Prospect House, Upton, Didcot, Berkshire. *8, 9, 14, 78.*

ALEXANDER, Joan *see* WETHERELL-PEPPER, Joan G.

ALLEN OF HURTWOOD, Lady (Marjory), F.I.L.A., Landscape Architect. **BEXLEYHEATH,** Kent, 10 May 1897. Author of "Gardens", "Whose Children?", "Adventure Playground", "The New Small Garden", "Play Parks", "Design for Play", "Planning for Play", "New Playgrounds", etc. 10 Selwood Terrace, London SW7. *1, 8, 31, 32.*

ALLEN, Clifford E(dward), M.D.(London), F.R.C.Psych., M.R.C.P., D.P.M., Consultant Psychiatrist (retired). **GRAVESEND,** Kent, 23 October 1902. *Founder Fellow, Royal College of Psychiatrists.* The Lodge, Llwyn Offa, near Mold, Flintshire, Wales. *6, 8, 9, 62.*

APPLETON, Carol Lavendder. **SHEERNESS,** Kent, 14 November 1935. Maesteilo, Capel Isaac, Llandeilo, Carmarthenshire, Wales. *62.*

APPS, Edwin, Actor and Author. **WINGHAM,** Kent, 1931. Author of "The Bishop Rides Again" (with Pauline Devaney), "All Gas and Gaiters", etc. 2a Talbot Place, Blackheath, London SE3. *8.*

ARKELL, A(nthony) J(ohn), M.B.E., M.C., D.Litt.(Oxon.), F.S.A., Archaeologist (retired). **HINXHILL,** near Ashford, Kent, 29 July 1898. Publications include: "Early Khartoum", "Shaheinab", "History of the Sudan", "Wanyanga", "The Old Stone Age in the Anglo-Egyptian Sudan", etc. Cuddington, Colam Lane, Little Baddow, Chelmsford, Essex. *1, 8.*

ARMSTRONG, J(ack) R(oy), M.A.(Hons.)(Oxon.), Senior Lecturer, Southampton University (retired). **BROADSTAIRS,** Kent, 22 August 1902. *Hon. Research Director, Weald and Downland Open Air Museum, Singleton, near Chichester, Sussex.* Author of "History of Sussex". Highover, Bracken Lane, Storrington, Sussex. *8, 81.*

ARNOLD, Ralph Crispian Marshall, B.A.(Oxon.), retired Publisher. **MEOPHAM,** Kent, 1906. Publications include: "A Very Quiet War", "Orange Street and Brickhole Lane", "The Unhappy Countess", "Northern Lights", "The Story of Lord Derwentwater", "The Whiston Matter", "Kings, Bishops, Knights and Pawns", "A Social History of England 55 B.C. *to* 1215 A.D.", "The Hundred of Hoo", "A Yeoman of Kent", "Spring List", "House with the Magnolias", "Hands Across the Water", etc. Swerford Old Rectory, Oxford.   *8.*

ASHBEE, Paul, M.A., F.S.A., Archaeologist. **MAIDSTONE,** Kent, 1918. *Secretary of the Centre of East Anglian Studies, University of East Anglia (since 1969).* Author of "The Bronze Age Round Barrow in Britain", "The Earthen Long Barrows", etc. The Old Rectory, Chedgrave, Norwich, Norfolk NOR 2OW.   *8.*

ATKINSON, Basil Ferris Campbell, M.A., Ph.D., Under-Librarian, University of Cambridge (1925–1960). **TUNBRIDGE WELLS,** Kent, 1895. Publications include: "Greek Language", "Valiant in Fight", "War with Satan", "Pocket Commentary on the Bible", "Christian's Use of the Old Testament", etc. 6 Highsett, Hills Road, Cambridge. *8, 9.*

AULD, William, M.A., Schoolmaster. **ERITH,** Kent, 6 November 1924. 20 Harviestoun Road, Dollar, Clackmannanshire, Scotland.   *63.*

BAGNOLD, Enid (Lady Jones), F.R.S.L., Playwright and Novelist. **ROCHESTER,** Kent, 27 October 1889. *Recipient of Award of Merit Medal, American Academy of Arts and Letters (1956) for "The Chalk Garden".* Publications include: "National Velvet", "The Chalk Garden", "The Chinese Prime Minister", "The Loved and Envied", "Enid Bagnold's Autobiography", etc. North End House, Rottingdean, Sussex BN2 7HA.   *1, 2, 8, 9, 53, 81.*

BAILEY, Cecil Henry, M.Sc.(London), Principal Lecturer, Didsbury Training College (retired). **BROCKLEY,** Kent, 1899. The Flags, 196 Chester Road, Hazel Grove, Cheshire.   *8, 66.*

BALDWIN, Michael, College Lecturer. **GRAVESEND,** Kent, 1930. Publications include: "The Silent Mirror", "Voyage from Spring", "Poetry Without Tears", "Grandad with Snails", "A World of Men", "Miraclejack", "Death on a Live Wire", "Poetry by Children", "In Step with A Goat", etc. 18 Sydney Road, Richmond, Surrey.   *8.*

14

BARCLAY, Brigadier C(yril) N(elson), C.B.E., D.S.O., Army Officer (retired). **DARTFORD,** Kent, 20 January 1896. *Editor, The Army Quarterly and Defence Journal (1950-1966); Army Editor, Brassey's Annual, The Armed Forces Year Book (1950-1967); Military Adviser to The Encyclopaedia Britannica (London Office).* Author of: "The History of the Cameronians (Scottish Rifles), 1933–1946", "The London Scottish in the Second World War, 1939 to 1945", "History of the Royal Northumberland Fusiliers in the Second World War", "The History of The Duke of Wellington's Regiment, 1919 to 1952", "The Regimental History of the 3rd Queen Alexandra's Own Gurkha Rifles, 1927–1947", "The History of the Sherwood Foresters, 1919–1957", "History of the 16th/5th The Queens Royal Lancers, 1925–1961", "The First Commonwealth Division" (Korea 1950–53), "The History of the 53rd (Welsh) Division in the Second World War", "The New Warfare", "Against Great Odds" (The Story of the first offensive in Libya in 1940–1941), "Battle 1066", "Armistice 1918", "Part-Time Farmer", etc. 44 Painters Field, St. Cross, Winchester, Hampshire. *1, 6, 7, 8, 9, 78.*

BARNARD, L(eslie) W(illiam), M.A.(Oxon.), Ph.D.(Southampton), University Lecturer. **BROMLEY,** Kent, 22 January 1924. *Leverhulme Research Fellowship (1957).* Publications include: "Studies in the Apostolic Fathers and Their Background", "C. B. Moss: Defender of the Faith", "Justin Martyr: His Life and Thought". 3 Carlton Road, Harrogate, Yorkshire. *8, 58.*

BARNES, Melvyn (Peter Keith), A.L.A., M.I.L.G.A., Librarian **RAMSGATE,** Kent, 26 September 1942. *Hon. Publications Officer, Association of Assistant Librarians. Author of "Youth Library Work".* Central Library, School Street, Newcastle, Staffordshire ST5 1AT. *8, 66.*

BAXTER, Gillian (Jose Charlotte), Riding School Instructor. **DARTFORD,** Kent, 1938. Author of "Horses and Heather", "Jump to the Stars", "Tan and Tarmac", "The Difficult Summer", "Ribbons and Rings", "The Stables at Hampton", "Horses in the Glen", "The Real Book of Horses", etc. 4 The Dower House, Gatton Park, near Reigate, Surrey. *8.*

BELL, Peter Robert, M.A., University Professor. **BEXLEYHEATH,** Kent, 1920. Publications include: "Darwin's Biological Work", "The Diversity of Green Plants" (in collaboration), etc. 13 Granville Road, Barnet, Hertfordshire. *8.*

15

BENNETT, Major Charles Moon, A.C.P., M.R.S.T., Headmaster (retired). **CANTERBURY,** Kent, 1899. Publications include: "Hereward the Wake", "Pedro of the Black Death", "Mutiny Island", "A Buccaneer's Log", "With Morgan on the Main", "Tim Kane's Treasure", "Red Pete the Ruthless", "Rivals of Camperdown School", "Camperdown Captains", "Easy Mathematics", "Civic English", " Spell, Speak and Write", "Happy English", "Read and Make", "Masters and Masterpieces", "You and Your World", "Captain Shrimp", "Meet the Magnets", "Find the Treasure", "A Most Amazing Property-Box", "Real Life English", etc. 106 Clay Hill, Enfield, Middlesex. *8, 9.*

BENSON, James, M.A.(Cantab.), Company Chairman. **BROMLEY,** Kent, 1925. Publications (with C. E. T. Warren) include: "Above Us The Waves", "The Admiralty Regrets . . .", "Will Not We Fear", "The Broken Column", etc. High Paddocks, Lye Green, near Crowborough, Sussex. *8, 81.*

BENSON, Stephana Vere, M.B.O.U. **BROMLEY,** Kent, 1909. *Founder and Hon. Secretary, Bird-Lovers' League.* Publications include: "The Observer's Book of Birds", "Birds at Sight", "Spotting British Birds", "The Child's Own Book of Prayers and Hymns", "The Greatest of These", "Birds of Lebanon and the Jordan Area", etc. 26 Downs View, Bude, Cornwall. *8.*

BIDDISS, Michael D(enis), M.A., Ph.D.(Cantab.), Fellow and Director of Studies, Downing College, Cambridge. **FARNBOROUGH**, Kent, 15 April 1942. Publications include: "Father of Racist Ideology: the Social and Political Thought of Count Gobineau", "Gobineau: Selected Political Writings" (Editor), "Disease and History" (Collaborator with F. F. Cartwright), etc. Downing College, Cambridge. *8.*

BISHOP, I(an) B(enjamin), M.A., B.Litt.(Oxon.), Lecturer in English. **GILLINGHAM,** Kent, 18 April 1927. Publications include: " 'Pearl' in its Setting: A Critical Study of the Structure and Meaning of the Middle English Poem", etc. University of Bristol, Department of English, 40 Berkeley Square, Bristol BS8 1HY, Gloucestershire. *8.*

BONHAM-CARTER, Victor, M.A.(Cantab.), Secretary of The Royal Literary Fund. **BEARSTED,** Kent, 1913. *Planning and Publications*

16

Officer, The Society of Authors, etc. Publications include: "The English Village", "Dartington Hall", "In a Liberal Tradition", "Farming the Land", "Soldier True", "Surgeon in the Crimea", etc. East Anstey, Tiverton, Devon. *8, 9, 79.*

BOOKER, Frank, Journalist. **SHOREHAM,** Kent, 1909. Publications include: "Industrial Archaeology Tamar Valley", "Wreck of the Torrey Canyon", "History of Morwellham", etc. 27 Widey Lane, Crownhill, Plymouth, Devon. *8, 79.*

BOX, Sydney, Author and Film Producer. **BECKENHAM,** Kent, 29 April 1907. Publications include: "Not This Man", "Diary of a Dropout", "The Golden Girls", etc. 42 Welbeck Street, London W1. *1, 8.*

BROADHURST, Brigadier R(onald) J(oseph) C(allender), Soldier and Orientalist. **SIDCUP,** Kent, 25 December 1906. *Sometime Assistant Chief of Staff, Arab Legion.* Publications include: "The Travels of Ibn Jubayr", etc. Belvedere, Ballyaughlis, Co. Down, Northern Ireland. *8, 9, 10.*

CAESAR, Dick, B.A.(Cantab.). **MAIDSTONE,** Kent, 1905. Author of "The Gobbling Billy" (With William Mayne), etc. Lime Ridge, Clapton-in-Gordano, Somerset. *8, 79.*

CALVER, Gordon Anthony, F.I.B., Banker. **BROMLEY,** Kent, 1921. Publications include: "The Banker's Guide to the Marine Insurance of Goods" (with Victor Dover), "Iran—Economic Review", etc. c/o The British Bank of the Middle East, 20 Abchurch Lane, London EC4. *8.*

CAMERON, D. Y. *see* COOK, Dorothy Mary (Jon Cook)

CAMERON-PRICE, George William James, Congregational Minister. **TUNBRIDGE WELLS,** Kent. Zion Hill Manse, Cuffs Lane, Tisbury, Wiltshire. *8, 78.*

CARLTON, Ann *see* TRENT, Ann.

CASS, Joan E(velyn), University Lecturer (retired). **SOUTHFLEET,** Kent. Publications include: "The Patchwork Quilt and other Poems", "Literature and the Young Child", 6 picture story books, etc. 9 Walcot Gardens, London SE11 6RB. *8, 9.*

CAWSTON, Lieut.-Col. E(dward) P(ercy), M.A.(Cantab.), LL.B., Author. **BROMLEY,** Kent, 15 July 1882. *Organiser, Editor, etc., Kent and Sussex Authors Conclave.* Publications include: "Lyrics and Legends in Kent and Sussex", "The Truth About Rhodesia", "Historical Notes on Bromley Hill", "The Plight and Flight of Christopher Marlowe", "Early Days at Eastbourne College", "Practical Entrenchments", "Practical Reconnaissance", "Machine Gunner in Flanders", "John Walker Arctic", "London Territorials in the Kaiser War", etc. Editor of "Canterbury Quartos". 11 Woodville Road, Bexhill, Sussex. *81.*

CHADWICK, Very Rev. Henry, D.D., Mus.B., F.B.A., Dean of Christ Church, Oxford. **BROMLEY,** Kent, 23 June 1920. Publications include: "Origen, Contra Celsum", "Alexandrian Christianity" (with J. E. L. Oulton), "Lessing's Theological Writings", "The Sentences of Sextus", "The Circle of the Ellipse", "St. Ambrose on the Sacraments", "The Vindication of Christianity in Westcott's Thought", "Early Christian Thought and the Classical Tradition", "The Early Church", "The Treatise on the Apostolic Tradition of St. Hippolytus of Rome", edited G. Dix (revised), "The Enigma of St. Paul", "Reflections on Conscience", etc. The Deanery, Christ Church, Oxford. *1, 8, 15.*

CHADWICK, (William) Owen, Hon.D.D.(St. Andrews), Hon.D.Litt. (Kent), F.B.A., Master of Selwyn College, and Regius Professor of Modern History. **BROMLEY,** Kent, 20 May 1916. Publications include: "John Cassian", "The Founding of Cuddesdon", "From Bossuet to Newman", "Western Asceticism", "Creighton on Luther", "Mackenzie's Grave", "The Mind of the Oxford Movement", "Victorian Miniature", "The Reformation", "The Victorian Church" (2 vols.), etc. Master's Lodge, Selwyn College, Cambridge. *1, 6, 7, 8, 9, 15.*

CHAPMAN R(ichard) A(rnold), B.A.(Leicester), M.A.(Carleton), Ph.D. (Leicester), A.M.B.I.M., University Reader in Politics. **BEXLEY-HEATH,** Kent, 15 August 1937. Publications include: "Decision Making", "The Higher Civil Service in Britain"; "Style in Administration" and "Readings in British Public Administration" (edited in collaboration), etc. University of Durham, Department of Politics, 23-26 Old Elvet, Durham. *8.*

18

CHRIMES, Stanley Bertram, M.A.(London), Ph.D., Litt.D.(Cantab.), University Professor. **SIDCUP,** Kent, 23 February 1907. *Fellow, Royal Historical Society, Alexander Silver Medal, 1934; Hon. President, Cardiff Branch, Historical Association; Vice President, Glamorgan History Society.* University College, Cathays Park, Cardiff, Wales. *1, 6, 7, 8, 9, 62.*

CHURCHILL, Reginald Charles, M.A.(Cantab.), Author and Journalist. **BROMLEY,** Kent, 9 February 1916. Publications include: "He Served Human Liberty", "Disagreements", "The English Sunday", "A Short History of the Future", "Shakespeare and His Betters", "Sixty Seasons of League Football", "The Powys Brothers", "Concise Cambridge History of English Literature" (with George Sampson), etc. 95 Collinswood Drive, St. Leonards-on-Sea, Sussex. *8, 10, 81.*

CLARE, Elizabeth *see* COOK, Dorothy Mary (Jon Cook).

CLARK, John Grahame Douglas, C.B.E., M.A., Ph.D., Sc.D.(Cantab.), Hon.D.Litt.(Sheffield), F.B.A., M.R.I.A., Disney Professor of Archaeology, Cambridge. **SHORTLANDS,** Beckenham, Kent, 28 July 1907. *Member, Ancient Monuments Board, 1954; Hon. Editor, Proceedings Prehistoric Society, 1935–1970; Member, Royal Commission on Historical Monuments, 1957–1969; President, Prehistoric Society, 1958–1962; Vice-President, Society of Antiquaries, 1959–1962, etc.* Publications include: "The Mesolithic Settlement of Northern Europe", "Archaeology and Society", "Prehistoric England", "From Savagery to Civilization", "Prehistoric Europe, The Economic Basis", "Excavations at Star Carr", "The Study of Prehistory", "World Prehistory, An Outline", "Prehistoric Societies" (with Stuart Piggott), "The Stone Age Hunters", "World Prehistory, a new outline", "Aspects of Prehistory", etc. 19 Wilberforce Road, Cambridge. *1, 8, 9.*

CLARK, Laurence (Walter), M.A.(Cantab.), Author. **MAIDSTONE,** Kent, 16 May 1914. Publications include: "39 Preludes", "Kingdom Come", "More than Moon", "Murder of the Prime Minister", "A Father of the Nation", etc. 6 Temple Gardens, Rickmansworth, Hertfordshire. *8, 9, 10, 14.*

CLEMENTS, Julia *see* SETON, Lady (Julia).

COLLEDGE, J(ames) J(oseph), Schoolmaster. **CHATHAM,** Kent, 18 January 1908. Publications include: "Warships of World War II" (with H. T. Lenton), "British Sailing Warships", "Ships of the Royal Navy" (2 vols.), "British Warships 1914–19" (with F. J. Dittmar), etc. 20 Hereford Road, Wanstead, London E11 2EA. *8.*

COLLINS, Canon Lewis John, M.A.(Cantab.), Clergyman. **HAWK-HURST,** Kent, 23 March 1905. *Awarded Order of Grand Companion of Freedom, (Third Div.) Zambia, 1970. Chairman, Christian Action, since 1946; Chairman, Martin Luther King Foundation, since 1969; President, International Defence and Aid Fund, since 1964.* Publications include: "The New Testament Problem", "A Theology of Christian Action", "Faith Under Fire", etc. 2 Amen Court, London EC4. *1, 8, 15.*

COLVIN, Howard Montagu, C.B.E., M.A., F.B.A., Hon.A.R.I.B.A., Senior Research Fellow and Librarian, St. John's College, Oxford. **SIDCUP,** Kent, 15 October 1919. *Member, Royal Fine Art Commission, since 1962; Royal Commission on Historical Monuments, since 1963; Historic Buildings Council for England, since 1970.* Publications include: "The White Canons in England", "A Biographical Dictionary of English Architects 1660–1840", "The History of the King's Works" (vols. 1 and 2 (with R. Allen Brown and A. J. Taylor)), "A History of Deddington", "Catalogue of Architectural Drawings in Worcester College Library", "Architectural Drawings in the Library of Elton Hall" (with Maurice Craig), "The Country Seat" (edited with John Harris), "Building Accounts of King Henry III", etc. 50 Plantation Road, Oxford. *1, 8.*

COOK, Dorothy Mary (Jon Cook), Insurance Employee. **GRAVESEND,** Kent, 13 February 1907. (*pseuds.* D. Y. Cameron, Elizabeth Clare) Publications include: "Enchanting Adventure", "Moonlight and March Roses", "A Royal Occasion", "Magic of Springtime", etc. 2 Penn Cottage, West End, Herstmonceux, Sussex. *9, 81.*

COOPER, Peter *see* FREEMAN, J(ohn) F(rederick).

CORNWELL, Edward Lewis, A.I.R.T.E., M.I.A.M., Technical Director. **SHOREHAM,** Kent, 1910. Author of "Commercial Road Vehicles", etc. 11 Fortescue Road, Weybridge, Surrey. *8.*

CORRIGAN P(hilip) R(ichard) D(ouglas), F.L.A., Lecturer, Librarian, and Writer. **PADDOCK WOOD,** Kent, 9 June 1942. *Theme Lecturer, International Conference on the Bibliographic Control of Library Science Literature, Albany, N.Y., 1968.* Publications include: "Education for Librarianship: a bibliography", "Introduction to Sears List of Subject Headings", etc. c/o Library Association, 7 Ridgmount Street, London WC1, or, St. Cuthbert's Society, Durham University, Durham City. *8, 54.*

COVENTRY, Rev. John Seton, M.A.(Oxon.), S.J., Lecturer in Theology. **DEAL,** Kent, 21 January 1915. Publications include: "Morals and Independence", "The Breaking of Bread", "Faith Seeks Understanding", "The Life Story of the Mass", "The Theology of Faith", etc. Heythrop College, Cavendish Square, London W1. *1, 8.*

CRAWLEY, Aidan M(erivale), M.B.E., M.A.(Oxon.), Politician, Company Director, Writer and Broadcaster. **BENENDEN,** Kent, 10 April 1908. *Sometime Member of Parliament; President, London Weekend Television.* Author of "Escape from Germany", "De Gaulle: A Biography". 19 Chester Square, London SW1. *1, 7, 8, 9.*

CRICHTON, Ruth M., B.A.(Hons.). Kent, 1914. *Member, Bradfield Rural District Council and Berkshire County Council.* Publications include: "From Croft to Factory" (with Dr. Gregory), "Commuters' Village", etc. The Red House, West End Road, Mortimer, Reading, Berkshire, RG7 3TH. *8, 78.*

CROSSE, Elaine *see* TRENT, Ann.

DALE, Norman *see* DENNY, Norman George.

DALZELL, William Ronald, A.R.C.A., Senior Art Master, Bedford School (1947–1970). **GRAVESEND,** Kent, 1910. Publications include: "Living Artists of the 18th Century", "Architecture the Indispensable Art", "Know the Gallery", "Architecture", etc. Bedford School, Bedford. *8.*

DEAN, Beryl, A.R.C.A., Ecclesiastical Designer and Embroiderer, Lecturer and Teacher. **BROMLEY,** Kent, 2 August 1911. Author of "Ecclesiastical Embroidery", "Church Needlework", "Ideas for Church Embroidery", "Creative Appliqué", etc. 27 Canonbury Grove, London N1 2HR. *8, 9.*

DENNY, Norman George, Author. Kent, 1901. (*pseud.* Norman Dale) Little Doccombe, Moretonhampstead, Devon. *8, 79.*

DERVENTIO *see* HUGHES, Walter Dudley.

DESANA, Dorothy *see* TRENT, Ann.

DESBOROUGH, V(incent) R(obin) d'A(rba), B.Litt., M.A.(Oxon.), F.B.A., F.S.A., Fellow of New College, Oxford. **TUNBRIDGE**

WELLS, Kent, 19 July 1914. Author of "Protogeometric Pottery", "The Last Mycenaeans and Their Successors", "The Greek Dark Ages", etc. 13 Field House Drive, Woodstock Road, Oxford OX2 7NT.   *1, 8.*

DEVLIN, Rt. Hon. Lord, P.C., Kt., M.A.(Cantab.), F.B.A., High Steward of Cambridge University. **CHISLEHURST,** Kent, 25 November 1905. *Recipient of several honorary doctorates.* Publications include: "Trial by Jury", "The Criminal Prosecution in England", "Samples of Lawmaking", "The Enforcement of Morals", "The House of Lords and the Naval Prize Bill", etc. West Wick House, Pewsey, Wiltshire.   *1, 8, 31, 32.*

DIPPER, Alan. **SHEERNESS,** Kent, 1922. Author of "The Wave Hangs Dark", "The Paradise Formula", "The Hard Trip", etc. Gate House, Beckley, near Rye, Sussex.   *8, 81.*

DUGGAN, Denise Valerie, Writer. **TONBRIDGE,** Kent. (*pseud.* Denise Egerton) Author of "No Thoroughfare", "A Man that I Love", Design for an Accident", "The Hour of Truth", "It Couldn't be Caroline", etc. 21 Fairmount Road, Bexhill-on-Sea, Sussex.   *8, 81.*

DUKE, Neville (Frederick), D.S.O., O.B.E., D.F.C., A.F.C., M.C. (Czech.), F.R.S.A., Company Director and Test Pilot. **TONBRIDGE,** Kent, 11 January 1922. Publications include: "Sound Barrier", "Test Pilot", "Book of Flying", "Book of Flight", "The Crowded Sky" (anthology), etc. The Old Fords, Northchapel, Sussex.   *1, 8, 81.*

EDGERLEY, John Torriano, M.A.(Cantab.), Barrister-at-Law, **WEST-GATE-ON-SEA,** Kent, 1904. 16 Porchester Terrace, London W2.   *8.*

EDWARDS, Michael John, B.A., Journalist, Translator and Photographer. **TONBRIDGE,** Kent, 1943. 165 Amesbury Avenue, London SW2.   *8.*

EGERTON, Denise *see* DUGGAN, Denise Valerie.

ENGHOLM, Eva, M.A.(Cantab.), **BECKENHAM,** Kent, 1909. Publications include: "Education through English", "Practical English for the Foreign Student", "Company of Birds", etc. Lame Ducks, Catsfield, Sussex.   *8, 81.*

ENSOR, (Alick Charles) David, Journalist and Author. **SHEERNESS,** Kent, 27 November 1906. *Member of Parliament for Bury and Radcliffe, 1964–1970.* Publications include: "Thirty Acres and a Cow", "I was a Public Prosecutor", "Verdict Afterwards", "With Lord Roberts through the Khyber Pass", etc. c/o National Westminster Bank Limited, 21 East Street, Chichester, Sussex. *1, 8, 81.*

EWING, Sir Alexander William Gordon, M.A.(Edinburgh), Ph.D.(Manchester), Hon.LL.D.(Manchester), Hon.Litt.D.(Ithaca, N.Y.), Professor Emeritus. **STOWTING,** Kent, 6 December 1896. *Knighted (1959); Hon. Fellow, Manchester Medical Society, etc. Co-author of several publications in the field of audiology and education of the deaf.* Horseshoe Cottage, Alderley Edge, Cheshire. *1, 32, 66.*

FAGG, Sidney Vernon, B.Sc., A.R.C.S., D.I.C., University Lecturer. **QUEENBOROUGH,** Kent, 12 April 1918. Author of "Differential Equations". University of Manchester Institute of Science and Technology, Sackville Street, Manchester, Lancashire. *8, 35.*

FAIRBAIRNS, Zoë (Ann), Student. **TUNBRIDGE WELLS,** Kent, 20 December 1948. Author of "Live as Family", "Down", etc. c/o A. M. Heath and Co., 35 Dover Street, London W1X 4EB. *8, 9.*

FERGUSON, Peter (Roderick) (Innes), B.A.(Oxon.), Lecturer. **BROMLEY,** Kent, 30 December 1933. *Book Society Recommendation (1959); Finalist, John Llewellyn Rhys Prize (1959).* Author of "Autumn for Heroes", "Monster Clough", "A Week Before Winter (In the Year of the Great Reaping)", etc. 74 West Riding, Bricket Wood, St. Albans, Hertfordshire. *8, 9, 10, 14.*

FISHER, Charles H(arold), C.Eng., F.I.Mech.E., M.S.A.E., Chartered Engineer. **SIDCUP,** Kent, Publications include: "Carburation" (2 vols.), "Carburation and Fuel Injection" (4 vols.), etc. Rowans, Shrewley Common, Warwick. *7, 8, 9, 14, 49, 74.*

FREEMAN, J(ohn) F(rederick), B.A., Schoolmaster. **MAIDSTONE,** Kent, 11 December 1937. *(pseud. Peter Cooper.) Past Chairman, Stockport Writers Circle.* 42 Ravenoak Road, Davenport, Stockport, Cheshire. *66.*

GALE, John, Journalist. **EDENBRIDGE,** Kent, 1925. Publications include: "Clean Young Englishman", "The Family Man", etc. 101 Oakwood Road, London NW11 6RJ. *8.*

GIESLER, Rodney William Aldous, Film Scriptwriter. **MANSTON,** Kent, 2 February 1931. *Winner of gold medal at the Atlanta International Festival, 1971, and silver medal at the International Film and Television Festival, New York, 1971, etc.* 41 Givons Grove, Leatherhead, Surrey, *8, 70.*

GLOVER, F(rank) Graham, M.A.(Oxon.), Barrister-at-Law. **GROVE PARK,** Kent, 13 May 1894. Publications include: "Gale on Easements" (edited), "Central & Local Government", "British Locomotive Design, 1825–1960", etc. Ripley Green Lodge, Ripley, Surrey. *8.*

GRANT, David (Ogilvie), B.A.(Hons.)(London), Schoolmaster. **BROMLEY,** Kent, 27 October 1925. *Awarded Arts Council Drama Bursary, 1962.* Author of "Waes" (novel), "From Classroom to Stage—Three New Plays", etc. 25 Dora Road, Wimbledon, London SW19. *8, 9.*

GREEVES, Rev. Frederic, B.A.(Manchester), M.A.(Cantab.), Hon. LL.D.(Bristol), Methodist Minister. **SIDCUP,** Kent, 1 June 1903. Author of "Jesus, the Son of God", "The Christian Way", "The Meaning of Sin", "Theology and the Cure of Souls", etc. 13 Eastmead Lane, Bristol 9, Gloucestershire. *1, 7, 8.*

GREGORY, Robin E(dward), B.A., Lecturer and Writer. **BARNEHURST,** Kent, 12 February 1931. *Editor, "Orbis", since 1969;* Author of "A Shorter Textbook of Human Development"; plays include "When the Wind Blows", "Long Live the King", "The Passing of Leena", etc. Rose House, Youlgrave, Bakewell, Derbyshire. *8, 66.*

GUIDO, (Cecily) Margaret, F.S.A., F.S.A.Scot., Archaeologist. **WEST WICKHAM,** Kent, 5 August 1912. *(pseud.* (formerly) C. M. Piggott) *Leverhulme Research Grant (1959), Central Research Grant, London University (1959).* Publications include: "Syracuse: A Handbook to its history and principal monuments", "Sardinia", "Sicily: An Archaeological Guide", "Southern Italy: An Archaeological Guide", etc. 3 Brock Street, Bath, Somerset. *8, 79.*

GUNTHER, Mavis, M.A. M.D.(Cantab.), Medical Research Worker. **SIDCUP,** Kent, 1903. Author of "Infant Feeding", etc. 77 Ember Lane, Esher, Surrey. *8.*

HADLOW, L(eonard) H(arold), B.A.(Hons.)(London), A.K.C., School-master. **RAINHAM**, Kent, 9 July 1908. *Past President (and now Vice-President), Manchester Branch of the Geographical Association.* Author of "Climate, Vegetation, and Man", "Asia" (with R. Abbott). 7 Merwood Avenue, Wilmslow Road, Long Lane, Cheadle, Cheshire. *8, 9, 66.*

HALE, John Rigby, M.A.(Oxon.), Fellow and Tutor in Modern History, Jesus College, Oxford. **ASHFORD**, Kent, 1923. Author of "England and the Italian Renaissance", "The Italian Journal of Samuel Rogers", "Machiavelli and Renaissance Italy", "The Literary Works of Machiavelli" (translator and editor), etc. 4 Rawlinson Road, Oxford. *8.*

HALE, Lionel (Ramsay), Journalist and Dramatist. Kent, 26 October 1909. Organiser of National Library Week, 1969. Publications include: "The Old Vic", "A Fleece of Lambs", etc. 76 Noel Road, London N1. *1, 8.*

HALL, Richard, M.A.(Oxon.), Editor. **MARGATE**, Kent, 1925. *Editor "The Observer" Colour Magazine, since 1970.* Publications include: "Kaunda, Founder of Zambia", "Zambia", "High Price of Principles", "Discovery Africa", etc. 47 Campden Hill Road, London W8. *8, 9.*

HAMMOND, Rev. Peter, M.A.(Oxon.), Clergyman and College Lec-turer. **BROMLEY**, Kent, 1921. Author of "The Waters of Marah", "Liturgy and Architecture", "Towards a Church Architecture", etc. 64 South Street, Cottingham, Yorkshire. *8, 15, 58.*

HAMPDEN, John, M.A.(Oxon.), Writer. **FOLKESTONE**, Kent, 6 February 1892. *Hon. Life Member, Society of Bookmen; Hon. Life Member, P.E.N.* Author of "Francis Drake, Privateer", "The Spanish Armada", "The Tudor Venturers", "Sea-Dogs and Pilgrim Fathers", "Books from Papyrus to Paperback", "The Book World Today", "Seventy-one Parrots", "The Yellow Dragon", "The Black Monkey", etc. Robin House, St. Mary's Terrace, Hastings, Sussex. *1, 8, 81.*

HARRISON, Michael, Journalist. **MILTON**, Kent, 1907. Publications include: "Weep for Lycidas", "Spring in Tartarus", "All The Trees Were Green", "Transit of Venus", "Dawn Express", "Vernal

Equinox", "Under Thirty", "What Are We Waiting For", "Gambler's Glory", "Count Cagliostro", "Battered Caravanserai", "Reported Safe Arrival", "So Linked Together", "Higher Things", "The House in Fishergate", "Mauritius, 1847" (stamp collecting), "Treadmill", "There's Glory for You", "Sinecure", "Long Vacation", "A New Approach to Stamp Collecting", "The Darkened Room" (with Douglas B. Armstrong), "The Brain", "Charles Dickens", "Airborne at Kitty Hawk", "The Dividing Stone", "Prince of Hokum", "Beer Cookery", "A Hansom to St. James's", "In the Footsteps of Sherlock Holmes", "The History of the Hat", "London Beneath the Pavement", "Painful Details", "Rosa", etc. c/o Laurence Pollinger Limited, Literary Agents, 18 Maddox Street, London W1R 0EU. *8.*

HEALEY, Rt. Hon. Denis (Winston), P.C., M.B.E., M.A.(Oxon.), M.P. **MOTTINGHAM,** Kent, 30 August 1917. Publications include: "The Curtain Falls", "New Fabian Essays", "Neutralism", "Fabian International Essays", "A Neutral Belt in Europe", "NATO and American Security", "The Race Against the H Bomb", "Labour Britain and the World", etc. House of Commons, Westminster, London SW1. *1, 8.*

HEATH, Rt. Hon. Edward (Richard George), P.C., M.B.E., Hon.D.C.L. (Oxon.), M.P., Prime Minister and First Lord of the Treasury (since 1970). **BROADSTAIRS,** Kent, 9 July 1916. Publications include: "One Nation a Tory approach to social problems" (joint), "Old World, New Horizons", etc. 10 Downing Street, London SW1. *1.*

HIGHAM, R. R. A., Editor and Joint Managing Director. Kent, 1935. Author of "A Handbook of Papermaking", "Paperboard and Board Manufacture" (2 vols.), "The Manufacture of Paperboard Containers", etc. Business Intelligence Services Limited, 79-80 Backfriars Road, London SE1. *8.*

HILL, Adrian (Keith) (Graham), R.O.I., R.B.A., R.I., Painter in Water Colours and Oils. **CHARLTON,** Kent, 1895. *President, Royal Institute of Oil Painters (1968); President, Chichester Society of Artists; Governor, Chichester School of Art (1951–1962); Governor of Midhurst Grammar School (1957–1967), etc.* Publications include: "On Drawing and Painting Trees", "On the Mastery of Water Colour Painting", "Art versus Illness", "Trees Have Names", "How to Draw", "The Pleasures of Painting", "Knowing and Painting Trees",

26

"Drawing the Countryside", "Adventures in Painting", "Seascapes and Landscapes", "Architecture in Landscape", "Further Steps in Oil Painting", "Introduction to Drawing and Sketching", etc. Old Laundry Cottage, Cowdray Park, Midhurst, Sussex. *1, 6, 7, 8, 9, 22, 81.*

HILL, B(arrington) J(ulian) W(arren), M.A.(Oxon.), F.I.A.L., Schoolmaster. **BROADSTAIRS**, Kent, 31 July 1915. Author of "Eton Medley", "Spanish Course", "History of Eton College", "Windsor and Eton", "Aural Composition in Spanish", "Cricket", "Football", "Background to Spain", etc. The Wall House, Eton College, Windsor, Berkshire. *8, 9, 10, 78.*

HODGES, Cyril Walter, F.S.I.A., Theatre Historian and Author. **BECKENHAM,** Kent, 1909. Author of "Columbus Sails", "The Flying House", "Shakespeare and The Players", "The Globe Restored", "The Namesake", "Shakespeare's Theatre", "The Marsh King", "The Norman Conquest", "The Spanish Armada", "Magna Carta", "The Overland Launch", etc. 15 Hill Rise, Bishopstone, Seaford, Sussex. *8, 9, 81.*

HOLLOM, Philip Arthur Dominic, F.A.C.C.A., Editor. **BICKLEY,** Kent, 1912. *Co-editor of "British Birds", since 1951.* Author of "The Popular Handbook of British Birds", "The Popular Handbook of Rarer British Birds", "A Field Guide to the Birds of Britain and Europe" (co-author), "Trapping Methods For Bird Ringers", etc. Crastock Cottage, Crastock, Woking, Surrey. *8, 9.*

HOYS, Frank Dudley. Kent, 1897. Publications include: "Below Scafell", "English Lakeland in Colour", "English Lake Country", etc. Also play: "Chinese White". The Woolpack, Eskdale, Cumberland. *8.*

HUGHES, Walter Dudley, Dip.Ed., Lecturer in Speech and Drama. **RAMSGATE,** Kent, 1918. (*pseud.* Derventio.) *Examiner, English Speaking Board.* Author of "Fish and Fishing", "There's More To Fishing", etc. 19 South Avenue, Littleover, Derby. *8, 66.*

HUNT, R(obert) W(illiam) G(ainer), D.Sc., Ph.D., D.I.C., A.R.C.S., F.R.P.S., M.R.T.S., F.I.O.P., F.R.S.A., Research Physicist. **SIDCUP,** Kent, 28 July 1923. Author of "The Reproduction of Colour". Research Laboratories, Kodak Limited, Harrow, Middlesex. *8, 9.*

HURST, Alexander Anthony. **BECKENHAM,** Kent, 1917. Publications include: "Ghosts on the Sea-Line", "The Call of High Canvas", "The Music of Five Oceans", "The Sailing Schoolships", etc. The Cedar House, Popeswood Road, Binfield, Berkshire.   *8, 78.*

JARVIS, Henry Wood. **TUNBRIDGE WELLS,** Kent, 1880. Author of "Let the Great Story be Told", "Pharaoh to Farouk", "The House of Silence", "The Forgotten Adventure", etc. 37 Regent Road, Surbiton, Surrey.   *8.*

JESSUP, Frank (William), C.B.E., M.A.(Oxon.), LL.B., F.S.A., Barrister-at-Law, Director, Department of External Studies, Oxford University. **HALLING,** Kent, 26 April 1909. Publications include: "History of Kent", "Sir Roger Twysden, 1595–1672", "Kent History Illustrated", "Lifelong Learning" (editor). Striblehills, Thame, Oxfordshire.   *8.*

JOHNSTON, Hamilton Charles Phillott, B.Sc., M.B., B.S. **SITTING-BOURNE,** Kent, 1915. Author of "The Doctor's Signature", "The Phantom Limb", "Dying Nicely", "The Fly in the Ointment", etc. 49 Thorne Road, Doncaster, Yorkshire.   *8, 58.*

JONES, Lady *see* BAGNOLD, Enid.

KEDWARD, H. R., M.A.(Oxon.), B.Phil., Lecturer in History, University of Sussex. **HAWKHURST,** Kent, 1937. *Leverhulme Research Fellow (1968–1969).* Author of "The Dreyfus Affair", "Fascism in Western Europe", etc. Arts Building, University of Sussex, Brighton, Sussex.   *8, 81.*

KENWARD, James Macara. **NEW ELTHAM,** Kent, 1 January 1908. Publications include: "Faber Junior Dictionary", "The Roof-Tree", "The Suburban Child", "Prep. School", etc. c/o Michael Joseph Limited, Publishers, 52 Bedford Square, London WC1B 3EF.   *8, 10.*

KIRK-GREEN, Anthony Hamilton Millard, M.B.E., M.A.(Cantab.), Senior Research Fellow, St. Antony's College, Oxford. **TUNBRIDGE WELLS,** Kent, 1925. Publications include: "Adamawa Past and Present", "Barth's Travels in Nigeria", "Principles of Native Administration", "Emirates of Northern Nigeria", "Hausa Proverbs", "Lugard and the Amalgamation of Nigeria", etc. St. Antony's College, Oxford.   *8.*

KIRK-GREENE, C(hristopher) W(alter) E(dward), M.A.(Oxon.), Schoolmaster. **TUNBRIDGE WELLS,** Kent, 19 July 1926. Publications include: "An Advanced French Vocabulary", "Sixty Modern French Unseens", "Les Mots-Amis et les Faux-Amis", etc. The College, Eastbourne, Sussex. *7, 8, 9, 81.*

LAMBERT, Michael, C.B.E. **BEXLEYHEATH,** Kent, 18 August 1907. *Awarded the "World's Paper Trade Review" Gold Medal, 1971. Member, National Joint Advisory Council for the Employment of the Disabled; Regional Industrial Tribunal (Bristol Area); National Advisory Council—City and Guilds of London Institute (Papermaking Courses). Until retirement, in 1972, Member of Council of the C.B.I., also Labour and Social Affairs Committee, Wages and Working Conditions Committee, Education Committee, International Labour Committee, National Safety Committee; Council of Employers' Federations of the European Free Trade Association (Papermaking Industry); Joint Advisory Council for the Prevention of Accidents in Paper Mills.* Publications include: "Industrial Relations in the Papermaking and Boardmaking Industry", etc. 28 Milton Abbas, Blandford, Dorset. *79.*

LANE, Michael, B.A.(Cantab.), Lecturer, University of Essex. **GILLINGHAM,** Kent, 1941. Author of "Books Girls Read", "Structuralism: A Reader", "Access to Higher Education", etc. 14 Broome Grove, Wivenhoe, Essex. *8.*

LANG-SIMS, Lois (Dorothy), Writer. **HERNE BAY,** Kent, 9 February 1917. Author of "The Presence of Tibet", "The Contrite Heart", "A Time to be Born", etc. Old Ford Cottage, Medbourne, Market Harborough, Leicestershire. *8.*

LEASOR, (Thomas) James, M.A.(Oxon.), Writer and Company Director. **ERITH,** Kent, 20 December 1923. Swallowcliffe Manor, Salisbury, Wiltshire. *1, 8, 9, 78.*

LESTER, Reginald Mountstephens, Editor. **HAWKHURST,** Kent, 1896. *Appointed Chairman, Council of The Churches' Fellowship for Psychical Study, 1953; President, Institute of Journalists, 1956–1957; Editor of "The Homefinder", 1946.* Publications include: "Everybody's Weather Book", "Weather Prediction", "Observer's Book of Weather", "Property Investment", "House Purchase", "The Householder and the Law", "In Search of the Hereafter", "Towards the Hereafter", "Building or Buying a House", "Practical Astronomy", "Estate Agents' Reference Handbook", "Air Training Course: Meteorology", etc. 5 Denison House, Vauxhall Bridge Road, London SW1. *8.*

LEWIS, Rev. Greville Priestley, B.A., B.D., Methodist Minister. **HERNE BAY,** Kent, 1891. *Connexional Secretary, Local Preachers' Department, 1946–1958; Director, "Methodist Recorder".* Publications include: "An Approach to the New Testament", "An Approach to Christian Doctrine" (editor), "The Johannine Epistles", "The Preacher's Handbook" (vols. 1–5), etc. 11 Parkway, Ratton Manor, Eastbourne, Sussex. *8, 81.*

LEWIS, M(arigold) J(oy), A.L.A., Lecturer in Librarianship. **BROADSTAIRS,** Kent, 15 May 1930. *Awarded Sevensma Prize, 1967.* Publications include: "Libraries for the Handicapped", "Reading Round the World" (with F. M. Gardner), etc. School of Librarianship, The Polytechnic of North London, 207–225 Essex Road, London N1 3PN. *8, 9.*

LIDDELL, (John) Robert, M.A., B.Litt.(Oxon.), F.R.S.L., Lecturer. **TUNBRIDGE WELLS,** Kent, 13 October 1908. Publications include: "Watering-Place", "The Last Enchantments", "Stepsons", "A Treatise on the Novel", "The Novels of Ivy Compton-Burnett", "The Novels of Jane Austen", "Mainland Greece", etc. c/o Barclays Bank Limited, High Street, Oxford. *1, 8, 9.*

LITTLE, Bryan Desmond Greenway, M.A.(Cantab.), Civil Servant (retired). **DEAL,** Kent, 1913. Author of "Building of Bath", "Cheltenham", "The Three Choirs Cities", "Exeter", "The Life and Work of James Gibbs", "Portrait of Cambridge", "Crusoe's Captain", "The Monmouth Episode", "Cambridge Discovered", "Bath Portrait", "Catholic Churches Since 1623", "Portrait of Somerset", "Cheltenham in Pictures", etc. c/o National Westminster Bank Limited, 32 Coin Street, Bristol, Gloucestershire. *8.*

LIVERTON, Joan. **BROMLEY,** Kent, 16 November 1913. (*pseud.* Joan Medhurst.) Publications include: "A Fragment of Beauty", "Cry Innocence", "The Shadowed Mirror", "R. X.", etc. Melai, Northiam, Sussex. *8, 81.*

LLOYD, John Phillip. **SIDCUP,** Kent, 1916. Publications include: "A.B.C. of Aircraft of World War One", "A.B.C. of R.A.F. Aircraft of World War Two", "A.B.C. of Historic Cars", "The Story of E.R.A.", "The World's Veteran to Vintage Cars", etc. Burcot Close, Burcot, near Abingdon, Berkshire. *8, 78.*

LONGMORE, Donald (Bernard), M.B., B.S., L.R.C.P., M.R.C.S.(Eng.), F.R.C.S.(Ed.), Surgeon. **BIRCHINGTON,** Kent, 20 February 1928. Publications include: "The Heart", "Machines in Medicine", "Spare Part Surgery", etc. 97 Chertsey Lane, Staines, Middlesex. *8.*

LOSTY, P. A., B.Sc., Ph.D., A.M.Inst.T., M.B.C.S. **FOLKESTONE,** Kent, 1924. Author of "Effective Use of Computers in Business", etc. 16 Neville Crescent, Bromham, Bedford. *8.*

MACFADYEN, Amyan, M.A., D.Sc.(Oxon.), F.Z.S., F.I.Biol. **WEALD,** Kent, 1920. Author of "Animal Ecology: Aims and Methods", "Secondary Productivity", etc. Mountpleasant, Mountsandel Road, Coleraine, Northern Ireland. *8.*

MACKENNA, F(rederick) Severne, M.A.(T.C.D.), M.B., B.Ch., B.A.O., F.S.A., F.S.A.Scot. **EDENBRIDGE,** Kent, 9 July 1902. Author of "Cookworthy's Plymouth and Bristol Porcelain", "Champion's Bristol Porcelain", "Chelsea Porcelain" (3 vols.), "Worcester Porcelain", "18th Century English Porcelain", "Catalogue of English Porcelain Collection" (3 vols.), etc. Dun Alasdair, Tarbert, Argyll, Scotland. *8, 63.*

MARCH, Edgar James, A.R.I.N.A. **RAMSGATE,** Kent, 1897. Author of "Spritsail Barges of Thames and Medway," "Sailing Drifters", "Sailing Trawlers", "British Destroyers", "Inshore Craft in days of Sail and Oar", etc. Green Acre, Colwell Bay, Freshwater, Isle of Wight. *8.*

MAY, Robin (Robert Stephen), Journalist and Writer. **DEAL,** Kent, 26 December 1929. Author of "Operamania", "Theatremania", "The Wit of the Theatre", etc. 23 Malcolm Road, London SW19 4AS. *8, 14.*

MEDHURST, Joan *see* LIVERTON, Joan.

MOGRIDGE, Stephen, Author. **BROADSTAIRS,** Kent, 1915. (*pseud.* Jill Stevens.) 62 Grosvenor Gardens, Bournemouth, Hampshire. *8, 78.*

31

MORRIS, Jean, B.A.(London). **SEVENOAKS**, Kent, 1924. *Awarded Arts Council Drama Bursary, 1955–1956.* Author of "Man and Two Gods", "Half of a Story", "The Adversary", "The Blackamoor's Urn", "A Dream of Fair Children", etc. 2 Langham House Close, Ham Common, Richmond, Surrey. *8.*

MORRIS, John (C. J. Morris), C.B.E., M.A., M.Sc. **GRAVESEND**, Kent, 27 August 1895. *Head of Far Eastern Service, BBC, 1943–1952, and Controller, Third Programme, 1952–1958, etc.* Publications include: "The Gurkhas" (with Major W. Brook Northey), "Handbooks for the Indian Army: Gurkhas", "Living with Lepchas", "Traveller from Tokyo", "The Phoenix Cup", "From the Third Programme" (edited), "Hire to Kill", "A Winter in Nepal", "Eating the Indian Air", etc. 21 Friday Street, Henley-on-Thames, Oxfordshire. *1, 8, 9.*

MYERS, Rollo H(ugh), M.A.(Oxon.), Officier d'Académie, Author and Musicologist. **CHISLEHURST**, Kent, 23 January 1892. Publications include: "Music in the Modern World", "Erik Satie" (biography), "Debussy", "Introduction to the music of Stravinsky", "Ravel: Life and Works", "Emmanuel Chabrier and his Circle", "Modern French Music", etc. Cobden Cottage, Queen Street, Eynsham, Oxford OX8 1HH. *8, 19, 27.*

NELSON, Michael (Harrington), Author and TV Interviewer. **YALDING**, Maidstone, Kent, 4 October 1921. (*pseud.* Henry Stratton.) Publications include: "Knock or Ring", "A Room in Chelsea Square", "When the Bed Broke", "Captain Blossom", "Blanket", etc. 42 Elsham Road, London W14. *8, 9.*

NEWMAN, Andrea, B.A.(London). **DOVER**, Kent, 1938. Author of "A Share of the World", "Mirage", "The Cage", "Three into Two Won't Go", "Alexa", "A Bouquet of Barbed Wire", etc. c/o Mrs. Robin Dalton, 4 Goodwin's Court, St. Martin's Lane, London WC2. *8.*

NICHOLLS, F(rederick) F(rancis), M.A.(Oxon.), Schoolmaster. **ROUGH COMMON**, Canterbury, Kent, 20 February 1926. Author of "Log of the Sardis", "The Free Traders", etc. Blackmore, Camrose, Haverfordwest, Pembrokeshire, Wales. *8, 9, 10, 62.*

NICOLSON, Lionel Benedict, C.B.E., M.V.O., Hon.Dr.R.C.A., Editor of "The Burlington Magazine", since 1947. **SEVENOAKS,** Kent, 6 August 1914. Publications include: "The Painters of Ferrara", "Hendrick Terbrugghen", "Wright of Derby: Painter of Light", etc. 45b Holland Park, London W11.   *1, 8, 9.*

NIXON, St. John Cousins, Motoring Correspondent. **BECKENHAM,** Kent, 1885. *Chairman, Guild of Motoring Writers, 1958.* Author of "The Invention of the Automobile", "Romance Amongst Cars", "Daimler 1896–1946", "Wolseley: a Saga of the Motor Industry", etc. Summerdown Cottage, Shere, Surrey.   *8.*

NOBBS, David Gordon, B.A.(Cantab), Author. **ORPINGTON,** Kent, 1935. Publications include: "The Itinerant Lodger", "Ostrich Country", "A Piece of the Sky is Missing", etc. 195 High Street, Barnet, Hertfordshire.   *8.*

NORRIE, Ian, Bookseller. **SOUTHBOROUGH,** Kent, 1927. Publications include: "The Book of Hampstead" (editor, with Mavis Norrie), "The Book of the City" (editor), "The Heathside Book of Hampstead and Highgate", "Hackles Rise and Fall", etc. 31 Granville Road, London N12.   *8, 9.*

OAKLEY, Eric Gilbert. **GILLINGHAM,** Kent, 1916. Author of "Success Through Self-Analysis", "Nature Cure Plan for Nerves", "Phial and Error", "Your Mind Matters", "How to Cultivate Confidence and Promote Personality", "Better Health from Health Foods and Herbs", etc. Flat 3, 25 Putney Hill, Putney, London SW15.   *8.*

OATEN, E(dward) F(arley), M.A.(Cantab.), LL.B., Barrister-at-Law, Director of Public Instruction, Bengal (retired).**TUNBRIDGE WELLS,** Kent, 24 February 1884. Author of "A Sketch of Anglo-Indian Literature", "European Travellers in India", "Glimpses of India's History", "Song of the Aton and other Poems", etc. 9 Beech Close, Walton-on-Thames, Surrey.   *1, 7, 8, 9.*

ODLUM, Doris M(aude), M.A.(Oxon.), M.R.C.S., L.R.C.P., D.P.M., Dip.Ed., etc., Consultant Psychiatrist. **FOLKESTONE,** Kent, 26 June 1890. *Appointed Fellow, British Medical Association (1958).* Author of "Psychology, The Nurse and The Patient", "Journey Through Adolescence", "The Mind of your Child", etc. Ardmor, 11 Cliff Drive, Canford Cliffs, Poole, Dorset.   *1, 6, 7, 8, 9, 79.*

O'HARA, Kenneth. **WATERINGBURY,** Kent. Author of "A View to a Death", "Sleeping Dogs Lying", "Underhandover", "Double-Cross-Purposes", "Unknown Man Seen in Profile", "The Bird Cage", etc. c/o Hughes Massie Limited, Literary Agents, 69 Great Russell Street, London WC1B 3DH. *8.*

OLBY, Robert (Cecil), B.Sc., M.A.(Oxon), D.Phil., University Lecturer. **BECKENHAM,** Kent, 4 October 1933. Author of "Origins of Mendelism", "Charles Darwin", etc. Department of Philosophy, The University, Leeds, Yorkshire LS2 9JT. *8, 58.*

OSBORNE, Geoffrey, Journalist. **GRAVESEND,** Kent, 1930. Author of "The Power Bug", "Balance of Fear", "Traitor's Gait", "Checkmate for China", etc. Paguera, Stoneyfields, Easton-in-Gordano, Somerset. *8, 79.*

PARRIS, Leslie, B.A.(London), Assistant Keeper, The Tate Gallery. **MAIDSTONE,** Kent, 1941. Author of "The Pre-Raphaelites", "The Loyd Collection", "John Constable" (with Conal Shields), etc. c/o The Tate Gallery, London SW1. *8.*

PATTERSON, Sheila (Caffyn), M.A.(Hons.)(Oxon.), Ph.D.(London), Social Anthropologist (Research Fellow), Writer and Editor. **MAIDSTONE,** Kent, 30 March 1918. Publications include: "Colour and Culture in South Africa", "The Last Trek", "Dark Strangers", "Immigrants in Industry", etc. 8 Adelaide Crescent, Hove, Sussex BN3 2JU. *8, 9, 81.*

PETRIE, Flavia (Isabel), B.A.(Hons.)(London), Lecturer in the History of Art. **WROTHAM,** Kent, 27 June 1944. 39 Baalbec Road, London N5.

PIGGOTT, C. M. *see* GUIDO, (Cecily) Margaret.

POPE, Dudley (Bernard) (Egerton), Naval Historian and Author. **ASHFORD,** Kent, 29 December 1925. Publications include: "Flag 4", "The Battle of the River Plate", "73 North", "England Expects", "At 12 Mr. Byng Was Shot", "The Black Ship", "Ramage" (novel), "Guns", "Ramage and the Drum Beat" (novel), "Ramage and the Freebooters" (novel), "The Great Gamble", etc. c/o Peter Janson-Smith Limited, 31 Newington Green, London N16 9PU. *1, 2, 7, 8, 9, 10, 34.*

34

PURDAY, Herbert Frank Percy, B.Sc., M.I.Mech.E., Writer. **BROMLEY,** Kent, 1887. Author of "Diesel Engine Design", "Stream-line Flow", "Diesel Engine Designing", "Linear Equations in Applied Mechanics", etc. 13 Southdown Road, Southwick, Brighton, Sussex BN4 4FT. *8, 9, 81.*

RAVEN, Ruth M(argaret) (Janey), Housewife. **RINGWOULD,** Kent, 5 May 1895. Author of "Bible Lessons for the Sunday Nursery". The Hermitage, Lyddington, near Uppingham, Rutland. *8.*

ROGERS, Neville (William), B.A., D.Lit.(London), F.R.S.L., Professor of English. **MARGATE,** Kent, 5 January 1908. Member of *Committee, British-Italian Society, since 1947, also Keats-Shelley Memorial Association, since 1946.* Publications include: "Keats, Shelley and Rome", "Shelley at Work", "Italian Regional Tales of the Nine-teenth Century" (edited, with Archibald Colquhoun), "The Esdaile Poems" (edited), "Selected Poetry of Shelley" (edited and annotated), "Complete Poetical Works of Percy Bysshe Shelley" (4 vols., edited), etc. 22 Clavering Avenue, London SW13. *1, 8.*

ROTHWELL, Talbot, Screenwriter and Playwright. **BROMLEY,** Kent, 12 November 1916. The Paddock, Fulking, Henfield, Sussex. *8, 36, 70, 81.*

RUSSELL, Rev. John Leonard, M.A.(Cantab.), Ph.D., S.J., Priest and Lecturer in Philosophy. **WYE,** Kent, 1906. Author of "Science and Metaphysics", etc. Heythrop College, 11 Cavendish Square, London W1. *8, 9.*

RUSSELL, Martin (James), Journalist. **BROMLEY,** Kent, 25 September 1934. Crime novels include: "No Through Road", "No Return Ticket", "Danger Money", Hunt to a Kill", "Deadline", "Advisory Service", etc. 1 Rosehill Cottage, Perrymans Lane, Bur-wash, Sussex. *8, 81.*

RUST, Doris, Journalist. **CHARLTON,** Kent. Author of "A Week of Stories", "A Story a Day", "All Sorts of Days", "The Animals at Number Eleven", "The Animals at Rose Cottage", "Mixed Muddly Island", "Simple Tales for the Very Young", "A Dog Had a Dream", "Secret Friends", "A Melon for Robert", "Tales from the Pacific", "A Tale of Three Rivers", "Tales from the Australian Bush", "Tales of Magic from Far and Near", etc. 1 Seymour Court, Hampton Wick, Kingston-on-Thames, Surrey. *8, 9.*

RUTLEY, Cecily Marianne, Teacher. **CHALK,** Kent. Author of "The God of the Silver Bow", "Stories from American History", "Children of Other Days", "Tales of the Wild Folk", "Nature's Year", etc. c/o Macmillan and Co. Ltd., Publishers, 4 Little Essex Street, London WC2R 3LF.   *8.*

ST. JOHN, John, Publisher. **GILLINGHAM,** Kent, 7 February 1917. Author of "Roast Beef and Pickles", "A Trick of the Sun", "Surgeon at Arms" (with Daniel Paul), "Probation—The Second Chance", "Alphabets and Reading" (with Sir James Pitman). 40 Arkwright Road, London NW3 6BH.   *8.*

SCOTT, Christopher, F.L.A.S., A.R.I.C.S. **CANTERBURY,** Kent, 1930. Publications (with Amoret Scott) include: "A–Z of Antique Collecting", "Collecting Bygones", "Tobacco and the Collector", "Dummy Board Figures", "Antiques as an Investment", "The Collecting Book", "Discovering Staffordshire Figures", "Discovering Smoking Antiques", etc. Miltons, Stratfield Saye, Reading RG7 2BT, Berkshire.   *8, 78.*

SERNICOLI, Davide *see* TRENT, Ann.

SETON, Lady (Julia), F.R.H.S., Author and International Floral Art Judge. Kent, 10 April 1906. (*pseud.* Julia Clements.) Publications include: "Fun With Flowers", "Fun without Flowers", "101 Ideas for Flower Arrangement", "Party Pieces", "First Steps with Flowers", "The Julia Clements Colour Book of Flower Arrangements", "Flower Arrangements in Stately Homes", "Julia Clements' Gift Book of Flower Arranging", etc. 122 Swan Court, London SW3.   *1, 8.*

SEWTER, A(lbert) C(harles), B.Sc.(Econ.)(London), M.A.(Manchester), F.M.A., F.R.S.A., Reader in History of Art, University of Manchester. **BECKENHAM,** Kent, 29 November 1912. *Former Chairman, Manchester Institute of Contemporary Arts.* Author of "The Relation Between Painting & Architecture", "The Art of Fresco Painting", "Modern British Woodcuts and Wood-Engravings in the Whitworth Art Gallery", etc. History of Art Department, The University, Manchester, Lancashire.   *8, 22, 66.*

SHERLEY-PRICE, Rev. Lionel Digby, M.A., Clergyman. **BECKENHAM,** Kent, 1911. Author of "Saints of England", "Queen of Peace", "A History of the English Church", "Lent with St. Francis", "The

Life and Writings of St. Francis", "The Little Flowers of St. Francis", "The Coming of the Franciscans", etc. The Vicarage, West Cliff Road, Dawlish, Devon. *8, 15, 79.*

SIMPSON, D(avid) P(enistan), M.A.(Oxon.), Schoolmaster. **CANTERBURY,** Kent, 3 October 1917. Publications include: "Cassell's New Latin Dictionary", "First Principles of Latin Prose", "Writing in Latin" (in collaboration with P. H. Vellacott), etc. Eton College, Windsor, Berkshire. *9, 78.*

SOMERSET FRY, Peter George Robin Plantagenet, F.R.S.A., Head of Information Services, Council for Small Industries in Rural Areas. **TENTERDEN,** Kent, 1931. Author of "Mysteries of History", "The Cankered Rose", "Rulers of Britain", "They Made History", "The World of Antiques", "Antique Furniture", "Constantinople: the story of 1000 years of Byzantine History", "The Wonderful Story of the Jews", etc. The Cottage, Little Bardfield, Braintree, Essex. *8.*

SONDHEIMER, Janet Harrington, M.A., Ph.D.(Cantab.), University Teacher and Translator. **BECKENHAM,** Kent, 1922. Published translations include: "The Medieval World", "The Holy Roman Empire", "The World of the Norsemen", "The Decline of Rome", "French Rural History", etc. 51 Cholmeley Crescent, London N6. *8.*

SOUTHWOOD, Thomas R(ichard) E(dmund), Ph.D., D.Sc., A.R.C.S., F.I.Biol., F.L.S., F.Z.S., F.R.E.S., Professor of Zoology and Applied Entomology, University of London. **NORTHFLEET,** Kent, 20 June 1931. *Awarded Forbes Memorial Medal (1952), Huxley Gold Medal (Imperial College) (1960), Scientific Medal (Zoological Society) (1969),* Publications include: "Land and Water Bugs of the British Isles", "Life of the Wayside and Woodland", "Ecological Methods", "Insect Abundance" (editor), etc. Imperial College, London SW7. *1, 8, 9, 14, 78.*

STANFORD, John Keith, O.B.E., M.C., M.A.(Oxon.), Company Chairman (retired). **BROMLEY,** Kent, 1892. Author of "The Twelfth", "Far Ridges", "Reverie of a Qu'Hai", "Mixed Bagmen", "Guns Wanted", "Bledgrave Hall", "Last Chukker", "No Sportsman At All", "Full Moon at Sweatenham", "A Bewilderment of Birds", "Fox Me", "British Friesians", "Jimmy Bundobust", "Death of a Vulpicide", "Broken Lanterns", "The Wandering Gun", "Ladies in

37

the Sun", "Tail of an Army", "The Complex Gun", "A Keepers Country", etc. c/o Lloyds Bank Limited, 6 Pall Mall, London SW1. *8, 9.*

STEPHENSON, William Lawrence, B.Sc.(Bristol), Electronic Engineer. **EASTCHURCH,** Kent, 1928. Author of "The Junction Transistor and its Applications" (in collaboration), etc. 41 Hevers Avenue, Horley, Surrey. *8.*

STEVENS, Jill *see* MOGRIDGE, Stephen.

STEWART, Rt. Hon. (Robert) Michael (Maitland), P.C., C.H., Hon. LL.D.(Leeds), M.P. **BROMLEY,** Kent, 6 November 1906. Author of "The Forty Hour Week", "Bias and Education for Democracy", "Policy and Weapons for the Nuclear Age", "The British Approach to Politics", "Modern Forms of Government", etc. 11 Felden Street, London, SW6. *1, 8.*

STRAKER, John Foster, Schoolmaster. **FARNBOROUGH,** Kent, 26 March 1904. Crime novels published include: "The Shape of Murder", "Ricochet", "Miscarriage of Murder", "Sin and Johnny Inch", "A Man Who Cannot Kill", "Tight Circle", "A Letter for Obi", "Hell is Empty" (subject of a film), etc. Lincoln Cottage, Horsted Keynes, Sussex. *6, 8, 9, 81.*

STRATTON, Henry *see* NELSON, Michael (Harrington).

SYKES, John B(radbury), M.A., D.Phil.(Oxon.), F.I.L., F.R.A.S., Lexicographer. **FOLKESTONE,** Kent, 26 January 1929, *Editor, Concise Oxford Dictionary, and Pocket Oxford Dictionary; Technical Translator's Manual. Since 1958, translator or joint translator of many Russian textbooks in physics and astronomy.* 20 Milton Lane, Steventon, Abingdon, Berkshire. *8, 9, 78.*

TATHAM, F(rancis) H(ugh) C(urrer), B.A.(Oxon.), Editor, Whitaker's Almanack. **GRAVESEND,** Kent, 29 May 1916. *Vice-Chairman, Society of Indexers.* 35 Little Common, Stanmore, Middlesex. *1, 8.*

TAYLOR, John G., B.Sc., M.A., Ph.D., University Professor. **HAYES,** Kent, 1931. Publications include: "Introduction to Quantam Mechanics", "The Shape of Minds to Come", "The New Physics", "Physics: An Introduction", etc. c/o International Authors Agency, Wadhurst, Sussex. *8, 9, 81.*

38

TAYLOR, John Russell, M.A.(Cantab.), Film Critic. **DOVER,** Kent, 1935. Publications include: "Joseph L. Mankiewicz", "Anger and After", "Cinema Eye, Cinema Ear", "The Art Nouveau Book in Britain", "The Rise and Fall of the Well Made Play", "Anatomy of a Television Play", "Penguin Dictionary of the Theatre", "Look Back in Anger: A Casebook", "The Art Dealers", "Harold Pinter", "The Hollywood Musical", etc. 11 Hollytree Close, Inner Park Road, London SW19. *8.*

TAYLOR, Norman Gardiner, Architectural Model Maker. **AYLES-FORD,** Kent, 7 September 1919. Publications include: "Model Aeroplanes", "Model Motor Boats", "Model Racing Yachts", "Model Racing Cars", "Model Makers Workshop", "The Complete Book of the Model Aeroplane", "Model Power Boats", "Architectural Modelling and Visual Planning", "00 Model Railway Layout and Operation". 113 Kenley Road, Merton Park, London SW19 3DP. *8.*

TAYLOR, William, B.Sc.(London), Ph.D., Professor of Education and Director of the School of Education, University of Bristol. **CRAY-FORD,** Kent, 31 May 1930. *Chairman, European Committee on Educational Research, 1969–1971.* Publications include: "The Secondary Modern School", "Society and the Education of Teachers", "Towards a Policy for the Education of Teachers" (edited), "Educational Administration and the Social Sciences" (edited with G. Baron), "Heading for a Change", "Planning and Policy in Post Secondary Education", etc. 35 Berkeley Square, Bristol BS1 1JA. *1, 8.*

THIMAN, Eric Harding, D.Mus.(London), F.R.C.O., Hon.R.A.M., Professor of Music. **ASHFORD,** Kent, 12 September 1900. *Dean of the Faculty of Music, London University, since 1956; Professor, Royal Academy of Music, London, since 1931; Organist to the City Temple, London, since 1958.* 7 Edmunds Walk, London N2. *1, 8, 9, 19.*

TINNE, Dorothea, M.B.E., N.R.D., Animal Painter, Writer, and Illustrator. **HAWKHURST,** Kent, 1 June 1900. (*pseud.* E. D. Tinne.) Publications include: "Lure of Lakeland", "Cheeky and Coy", "Signposts to the Wild", "Adventurous Holidays", "Love and Laughter". High Wray, Lodge Hill Road, Farnham, Surrey. *1, 6, 7, 8.*

TINNE, E. D. *see* TINNE, Dorothea.

TRENT, Ann, F.I.A.L., Novelist. **GRAVESEND**, Kent. (*pseuds.* Elaine Crosse, Ann Carlton, Dorothy Desana, Davide Sernicoli.) Publications include: "No Other Love", "Love Under the Stars", "Lovers' Quest", "Escape to Romance", "My Love", "The Unguarded Moment", "The Road to Romance", "One Love For Ever", "Blessed Surrender", "Moonlight Beguiling", "Jewel of Destiny", "The Unforeseen Hazard", "The White Squadron", and some 26 earlier novels. Crosselands, Salisbury Road, Carshalton, Surrey. *8.*

TREVES, Frederick W(illiam), B.E.M., Actor. **CLIFTONVILLE,** Margate, Kent, 29 March 1925. *Recipient of Lloyds War Medal (1943), Korda Scholarship to RADA (1947), Emile Littler Prize at RADA (1948).* Publications include radio and TV plays, etc. c/o Kavanagh Entertainments Limited, 170 Piccadilly, London W1V 9DD. *8.*

TRUSSLER, Simon, M.A.(London), Author. **TENTERDEN**, Kent, 11 June 1942. *Arts Council Award, 1969. Editor of "Theatre Quarterly"; Editor of "The Oxford Companion to the Theatre".* Publications include: "Theatre at Work", "Burlesque Plays of the Eighteenth Century", "Eighteenth Century Comedy", "The Plays of John Osborne", "The Plays of Arnold Wesker", "The Plays of John Whiting", etc. Theatre Quarterly, 39 Goodge Street, London, W1P 1FD. *8, 9, 10.*

UNSTEAD, R(obert) J(ohn), Author. **DEAL,** Kent, 21 November 1915. *Headmaster, Grange School, Letchworth, Hertfordshire, 1947–1957.* Publications include: "Looking at History", "People in History", "Teaching History in the Junior School", "A History of Houses", "Travel By Road", "Looking at Ancient History", "Monasteries", "Some Kings and Queens", "Royal Adventurers", "A History of Britain", "Early Times", "Men and Women in History", "The Story of Britain", "Homes in Australia", "Transport in Australia", "Pioneer Home Life in Australia", "Castles", "Invaded Island", "Kings, Barons, Serfs"; Editor: Black's Junior Reference series, Children's Encyclopaedia, Looking at Geography, etc. Reedlands, Thorpeness, Suffolk. *1, 8, 9.*

URRY, W(illiam) G(eorge), M.A.(Oxon.), Ph.D.(London), F.S.A., F.R.Hist.S., Reader in Medieval Western Palaeography, University of Oxford, and Fellow of St. Edmund Hall. **CANTERBURY,** Kent, 17 December 1913. *Member of Council, Kent Archaeological Society, since 1945.* Author of "Canterbury under the Angevin Kings". St. Edmund Hall, Oxford.

VALENTINE, Donald Graham, M.A., LL.B.(Cantab.), Dr.Jur.(Utrecht), Reader in Law, London School of Economics. **SALTWOOD,** Kent, 1929. Publications include: "The Court of Justice of the European Coal and Steel Community", "The Encyclopaedia of Housing" (edited with Percy Lamb, Q.C.), "Common Market Law Reports" (editor), etc. The London School of Economics, Aldwych, London WC2. *8.*

WAKELEY, Sir Cecil (Pembrey Grey), Bart., K.B.E., C.B., D.Sc. (London), M.Ch., F.R.S.E., F.R.C.S., F.R.S.A., F.K.C., F.Z.S, Hon. F.R.C.S.E., Hon. F.R.F.P.S., etc., Consulting Surgeon **RAINHAM,** Kent, 5 May 1892. *Recipient of several honorary doctorates and foreign decorations. President, Royal College of Surgeons (1949–1954).* Woodlands, Cold Ash Hill, Liphook, Hampshire. *1, 8, 32, 78.*

WARD, Rev. Arthur Marcus, M.A., D.D., College Tutor. **SEVENOAKS,** Kent, 1906. Author of "Our Theological Task", "The Byzantine Church", "Outlines of Christian Doctrine" (2 vols.), "The Pilgrim Church", "Commentary on St. Matthew", "The Churches Move Together", "A Theological Book List, 1963, 1968, 1970", etc. The Field House, Richmond College, Surrey. *8.*

WELLS, George Philip, Sc.D., F.R.S., Emeritus Professor of Zoology in the University of London. **SANDGATE,** Kent, 17 July 1901. Publications include: "The Science of Life" (1929–1930, in fortnightly parts, with H. G. Wells and Julian Huxley); also many scientific and other writings. University College, London WC1. *1, 8.*

WETHERELL-PEPPER, Joan G., Writer. **SOUTHBOROUGH,** Kent, 21 July 1920. (*pseud.* Joan Alexander.) Publications include: "Fly Away Paul", "The Choice and the Circumstance", "Carola", "Lewis's Wife", "Thy People My People", "Where Have All The Flowers Gone?", "Strange Loyalty", "Bitter Wind", etc. Coachman's Cottage, 33 Grove Road, Barnes, London SW13. *6, 8, 9.*

WHISTLER, Laurence, C.B.E., B.A., F.R.S.L., Engraver on Glass and Writer. **ELTHAM,** Kent, 21 January 1912. *Awarded King's Gold Medal for Poetry (1935)—the first recipient of that award; recipient of Atlantic Award for Literature (1945).* Publications include: "Sir John Vanbrugh", "The English Festivals", "Rex Whistler, His Life and His Drawings", "The World's Room" (collected poems), "The Engraved Glass of Laurence Whistler", "Rex Whistler: The Königsmark Drawings", "The Imagination of Vanbrugh and his Fellow Artists", "The View From This Window" (poems), "Engraved Glass",

"The Work of Rex Whistler" (with Ronald Fuller), "Audible Silence" (poems), "The Initials in the Heart", "To Celebrate Her Living" (poems), etc. Little Place, Lyme Regis, Dorset. *1, 8, 9, 79.*

WHITE, John Henry, M.Sc., Ph.D., F.R.I.C., L.R.A.M., A.R.C.M., A.R.C.O., Schoolmaster and Organist (retired). **TUNBRIDGE WELLS,** Kent, 1906. Author of "Teaching Chemistry", "A Reference Book of Chemistry", " Inorganic Chemistry", "Extraction of Metals", etc. 35 St. James's Drive, London SW17. *8, 9.*

WILLIAMS, Cicely (Maud), Housewife. **CHATHAM,** Kent, 10 February 1907. Publications include: "Bishop's Wife—But Still Myself", "Zermatt Saga", "Dear-Abroad", "Diary of a Decade". Bishop's Lodge, Springfield Road, Leicester LE2 3BD.

WILLIAMS, Rt. Rev. Ronald (Ralph), M.A.(Cantab.), D.D.(Lambeth), Bishop of Leicester. **ORPINGTON,** Kent, 14 October 1906. Publications include: "Authority in the Apostolic Age", "Acts of the Apostles", "Letters of John James", "I Believe and Why", etc. Bishop's Lodge, Springfield Road, Leicester LE2 3BD. *1, 8, 15.*

WISKEMANN, Elizabeth, M.A.(Cantab.), D.Litt., University Teacher. **SIDCUP,** Kent. Author of "Czechs and Germans", "Undeclared War", "The Rome-Berlin Axis", "Germany's Eastern Neighbours", "A Great Swiss Newspaper", "Europe of the Dictators", "The Europe I saw", "Fascism in Italy", etc. 41 Moore Street, London SW3. *8.*

WREN, Wilfrid J., B.A.(Cantab.), L.M.S.S.A.(London), General Medical Practitioner. **BROMLEY,** Kent, 1930. Author of "The Tanat Valley: its Railways and Industrial Archaeology", etc. Rivendell, Waveney Hill, Oulton Broad, Lowestoft, Suffolk. *8.*

ZAEHNER, Robert Charles, M.A.(Oxon.), Hon.D.Litt.(Lancaster), F.B.A., Spalding Professor of Eastern Religions and Ethics, University of Oxford. **SEVENOAKS,** Kent, 8 April 1913. Author of "Foolishness to the Greeks", "Zurvan, a Zoroastrian Dilemma", "The Teachings of the Magi", "Mysticism Sacred and Profane", "At Sundry Times", "The Concise Encyclopaedia of Living Faiths" (editor), "Hindu and Muslim Mysticism", "The Dawn and Twilight of Zoroastrianism", "Hinduism", "The Convergent Spirit", "The Catholic Church and World Religions", "Hindu Scriptures", (editor and translator), "The Bhagavad-Gita", "Concordant Discord", "Evolution in Religion", "Dialectical Christianity and Christian Materialism", etc. All Souls College, Oxford. *1, 8.*

Authors born in Kent who are currently resident and / or working Overseas

ABBIE, Andrew Arthur, M.D., D.Sc., Ph.D., F.R.A.C.P., F.R.A.I., University Professor. **GILLINGHAM,** Kent, 1905. Author of "Principles of Anatomy", "Human Physiology", "The Original Australians", etc. 8 Elm Street, Unley Park, South Australia 5061. *8, 9.*

BURGESS, Trevor *see* TREVOR, Elleston.

CAPON, Rev. Anthony (Charles), M.A., B.D., Clergyman. **CHISLE- HURST,** Kent, 1926. *Assistant General Secretary, Scripture Union of Canada, 1956–1960, General Director, 1960–1970, Regional Secretary for the Americas, 1970 onwards.* Publications include: "The Church and the Child" (with Elizabeth Capon), etc. Scripture Union, 3 Rowanwood Avenue, Toronto 289, Ontario, Canada. *8, 15.*

CAWLEY, Arthur Clare, M.A., Ph.D., University Professor. **GILLING- HAM,** Kent, 1913. Publications include: "Everyman and Medieval Miracle Plays", "The Wakefield Plays in the Townely Cycle", "Chaucer's Canterbury Tales", "George Meriton's A Yorkshire Dialogue", "Everyman", "Pearl and Sir Gawain and the Green Knight", etc. Department of English, University of Queensland, Brisbane, Australia. *8.*

CONWAY, H(arry) D(onald), M.A., Sc.D.(Cantab.), B.Sc., Ph.D., D.Sc. (Eng.)(London), University Professor. **CHATHAM,** Kent, 3 December 1917. Publications include: "Aircraft Strength of Materials", "Mechanics of Materials", etc. Department of Mechanics, Thurston Hall, Cornell University, Ithaca, N.Y. 14850, U.S.A. *2, 8, 14, 44, 45.*

CROFT-COOKE, Rupert, B.E.M., Writer. **EDENBRIDGE,** Kent, 20 June 1903. Author of many publications including: "Some Poems", "Troubadour", "Give him the Earth", "Night Out", "Cosmopolis", "Release the Lions", "Picaro", "Shoulder the Sky", "Blind Gunner", "Crusade", "God in Ruins", "Kingdom Come", "The World is Young" (autobiography), "Rule Britannia", "Darts", "How to get more out of Life", "The Man in Europe Street" (autobiography), "Same Way Home", "The Circus has no Home" (autobiography), "Glorious", "Octopus", "Ladies Gay", "The Circus Book" (editor), "The Moon in My Pocket" (autobiography), "Rudyard Kipling", "Wilkie", "Brass Farthing", "Three Names for Nicholas", "Cities", "The Sawdust Ring", "Nine Days with Edward", "The Life for Me" (autobiography), "The Blood-Red Island" (autobiography), "Harvest Moon", "The Verdict of You All" (autobiography), "A Few Gypsies", "Fall of Man", "Sherry", "Seven Thunders", "The Tangerine House" (autobiography), "Port", "Barbary Night", "The Gardens of Camelot" (autobiography), "Smiling Damned Villain", "The Quest for Quixote" (autobiography), "The Altar in the Loft" (autobiography), "Thief", "The Drums of Morning" (autobiography), "English Cooking", "Madeira", "The Glittering Pastures" (autobiography), "Wine and Other Drinks", "The Numbers Game" (autobiography), "Bosie", "The Last of Spring" (autobiography), "The Wintry Sea" (autobiography), "Paper Albatross", "The Gorgeous East", "The Purple Streak" (autobiography), "The Wild Hills" (autobiography), "The Happy Highways" (autobiography), "Feasting With Panthers", "The Ghost of June", "The Sound of Revelry", "Wolf from the Door", "Exotic Food", "Exiles", "Under the Rose Garden", "While the Iron's Hot", "The Licentious Soldiery" (autobiography), etc. Glenageary House, Dun Laoghaire, Co. Dublin, Ireland. *1, 2, 6, 7, 8, 9, 16.*

ELPHINSTONE, Francis *see* POWELL-SMITH, Vincent.

GALLOWAY, Margaret Cecilia, A.R.C.M., Lecturer. **ROCHESTER,** Kent, 1915. Author of "Making and Playing Bamboo Pipes", "Suites for Purcell", "Making Music with Young Children", etc. Apartment 610, 1911 Victoria Park Avenue, Scarborough, Ontario, Canada. *8.*

HALL, Adam *see* TREVOR, Elleston.

JUSTICAR *see* POWELL-SMITH, Vincent.

KENNEDY, Reginald Frank, Hon.M.A., F.L.A., Librarian (retired). **PLUMSTEAD,** Kent, 1897. *City Librarian of Johannesburg (1936–1960); Editor, Africana Notes and News (1943–1960).* Publications include: "Journal of Residence in Africa, by Thomas Baines" (edited), "Africana Repository", "Classified Cataloguing", "Catalogue of Pictures in the Africana Museum" (5 vols.), "The Heart of a City", etc. 153 Jan Smuts Avenue, Parkwood, Johannesburg, Republic of South Africa. *8.*

KING, Albert. **ERITH,** Kent, 1906. Author of "Raw Materials for Electric Cables", etc. Santo Amaro de Oeiras, Portugal. *8.*

PERCY, Lt.-Commander Herbert Roland, R.C.N. (retired), Writer. **BURHAM,** Kent, 6 August 1920. *Member, Institute of Marine Engineers. Vice-President, Canadian Authors' Association; Editor, "Canadian Author and Bookman" (1963–1966).* Author of "The Timeless Island". Granville Ferry, Annapolis County, Nova Scotia, Canada. *8.*

POWELL-SMITH, Vincent, LL.M.(Birmingham), D.Litt.(Geneva), F.R.S.A., F.S.A.Scot., A.Ph.S., University Lecturer. **WESTERHAM,** Kent, 28 April 1939. (*pseuds.* Justicar, Francis Elphinstone, Santa Maria.) *Recipient: Grand Prix Huminitarie de France (1971); Officier, Merite—Devouement Francais (1971); Medaille de Vermeil, "Arts-Sciences-Lettres" (1971); Freeman, City of London (1967). Consejo Juridico Heraldico of Spain: Corresponding Member of the Heraldry Society.* Publications include: "The Law of Boundaries and Fences", "The Building Regulations Explained and Illustrated", "The Law and Practice relating to Company Directors", "Episcopal Heraldry in England and Wales", "Kings Across the Water", etc. Ara Caeli, 91 St. Luke's Street, Bugbibba, St. Paul's Bay, Malta. *7, 8, 10, 14, 50, 61, 64.*

RADDALL, Thomas H(ead), Hon.LL.D.(Dalhousie), Hon.Litt.D., Author. **HYTHE,** Kent, 13 November 1903. *Recipient of Governor-General's Award, 1944, 1948, 1957; Gold Medal, Royal Society of Canada, 1956; Service Medal, Order of Canada, 1970.* Publications include: "The Nymph and the Lamp" (novel), "The Path of Destiny" (Canadian history), and fifteen other novels, volumes of history, collected short stories, the latest being "Footsteps on Old Floors". 44 Park Street, Liverpool, Nova Scotia, Canada. *3, 8, 9.*

RATTRAY, Simon *see* TREVOR, Elleston.

RODD, John. **GREENHITHE,** Kent, 1905. Author of "The Repair and Restoration of Furniture". 1830 McMicken Road, R.R.1., Sidney, B.C., Canada. *8.*

SANTA MARIA *see* POWELL-SMITH, Vincent.

SCOTT, Warwick *see* TREVOR, Elleston.

SHEPHARD, Lieut.-Col. John Brownlow, Indian Army (retired). **HEVER,** Kent. Author of "Rooineks Ride", "Land of the Tikoloshe", etc. Little Stream, Swartberg, East Griqualand, Republic of South Africa. *8.*

SIMMS, Peter Francis Jordan, M.A.(Cantab.), Writer and Editor. **ORPINGTON,** Kent, 1925. Publications include: "The Treasures of a Kingdom", "The Irrawaddy", "Trouble in Guyana", etc. 67 Farnham Avenue, Toronto 7, Ontario, Canada. *8.*

SMITH, Caesar *see* TREVOR, Elleston.

SPICER, John Ronald. **LYNSTED,** Kent, 1923. Author of "Cry of the Storm-Bird", etc. c/o National Bank of Australasia, Goulburn, N.S.W., Australia. *8.*

TREVOR, Elleston, Author. **BROMLEY,** Kent, 17 February 1920. (*pseuds.* Adam Hall, Simon Rattray, Caesar Smith, Trevor Burgess, Warwick Scott.) *Recipient of U.S. Mystery Writers' Award, the "Edgar" in 1965, for "The Quiller Memorandum", also French Grand Prix de Littérature Policière, in 1965, for the same novel.* Publications include: "The Big Pick-Up", "Squadron Airborne", "The Killing-Ground", "The Freebooters", "Bury Him Among Kings", "Gale Force", "The Flight of the Phoenix", "The Quiller Memorandum", "The Ninth Directive", "The Striker Portfolio", "The Warsaw Document", etc. Domaine de Chateauneuf, 06 Valbonne, France. *1, 2, 6, 8, 9.*

WARD-PERKINS, John Bryan, C.B.E., M.A., F.B.A., F.S.A., Director of the British School at Rome. **BROMLEY,** Kent, 1912. *Recipient of honorary doctorates, etc.* Publications include: "London Museum Medieval Catalogue", "Inscriptions of Roman Tripolitania", "The Shrine of St. Peter", "The Great Palace of Byzantine Emperors" (jointly), "The Historical Topography of Veii", "The Northeastern Ager Veieintanus", "Etruscan and Roman Architecture" (jointly), etc. British School at Rome, 61 Via Gramsci, 00197 Rome, Italy. *1, 8.*

WINTER, Lewis Bland, M.A.(Cantab.), M.D., Physiologist. **CHART-HAM,** Kent, 1898. Author of "We Who Adventure", "Nor They Understand", etc. 50 Hamilton Street, Lane Cove. N.S.W., Australia. *8.*

Authors resident and/or working in Kent who were not born in the County

ADAMSON, Donald, B.Litt.(Oxon.), M.A., D.Phil., Senior Lecturer in French, Goldsmiths' College, London. **CULCHETH,** Lancashire, 30 March 1939. Publications include: "The Genesis of 'Le Cousin Pons' ", "Dusty Heritage: A National Policy for Museums and Libraries"; translated Balzac "The Black Sheep"; edited "T. S. Eliot: A Memoir" (by the late Robert Sencourt), etc. Dodmore House, The Street, Meopham, Kent DA13 0AJ. *8, 9, 14, 35, 64.*

AIRD, Catherine *see* McINTOSH, Kinn Hamilton.

AMBERLEY, Richard *see* BOURQUIN, Paul (Henry) (James).

ARMSTRONG, Sybil *see* EDMONDSON, Sybil.

ARTHUR, Frank. **LONDON,** 1902. *Vice-President, Society of Civil Service Authors (since 1969); Hon. Librarian, Crime Writers' Association (since 1969).* Publications include: "The Suva Harbour Mystery", "Another Mystery in Suva", "Murder in the Tropic Night", "The Throbbing Dark", "The Abandoned Woman: The Story of Lucy Walter (1630–1658)", etc. 106 Southborough Road, Bromley, Kent. *8, 9, 10.*

ASHBY, Gwynneth Margaret, Author and Lecturer. **BIRMINGHAM,** Warwickshire. Publications include: "Mystery of Coveside House", "The Secret Ring", "The Cruise of the Silver Spray", "The Land and People of Belgium", "The Land and People of Sweden", "Let's Look at Austria", "Looking at Norway", "Looking at Japan", etc. Yewdene, Den Cross, Edenbridge, Kent. *8, 9, 10.*

ASHFORD, Jeffrey *see* JEFFRIES, Roderic (Graeme).

ATKINS, Sir Hedley (John Barnard), K.B.E., K.St.J., D.M., M.Ch., F.R.C.S., F.R.C.P., Professor of Surgery. **LONDON,** 30 December 1905. Publications include: "After-Treatment", "Tools of Biological Research" (editor), "The Surgeon's Craft", etc. Down House, Downe, Kent BR6 7JT. *1, 8, 9.*

BADGER, Alfred Bowen, M.A.(London), Ph.D.(Hamburg), Writer and Lecturer. **LLANELLI,** Carmarthenshire, Wales, 1901. Author of "Public Schools and the Nation", "Man in Employment", etc. 10 Parkside, 14 Court Downs Road, Beckenham, Kent. *8, 62.*

E   51

BANNER, Major E(dgar) H(arold) W(alter), T.D., M.Sc., C.Eng., F.I.E.E., F.I.Mech.E., F.Inst.P., Electrical Engineer, Author and Editor. **KINGS NORTON,** Birmingham, Warwickshire, 24 November 1897. Publications include: "Electronic Measuring Instruments", "Electrical Measuring Instrument Practice", "The Modern Electrical Engineer" (editor and part author), etc. Claydene, Cowden, Edenbridge, Kent, *8, 14, 29.*

BARFIELD, (Arthur) Owen, B.C.L., M.A., B.Litt.(Oxon.), Hon.H.L.D. (U.S.A.), F.R.S.L., Solicitor (retired). **LONDON,** 1898. (*pseud.* G. A. L. Burgeon) Publications include: "History in English Words", "Poetic Diction: A Study in Meaning", "Romanticism Comes of Age", "This Ever Diverse Pair", "Saving the Appearances: A Study in Idolatry", "Worlds Apart", "Unancestral Voice", "Speaker's Meaning", "What Coleridge Thought", etc. Orchard View, Gills Road, South Darenth, near Dartford, Kent. *8, 9, 10.*

BARKER, Eric (Leslie), Author, Actor and Broadcaster. **THORNTON HEATH,** Surrey, 20 February 1912. Publications include: "The Watch Hunt", "Day Gone By", "Steady Barker" (autobiography), "Golden Gimmick", etc. c/o Lloyds Bank Limited, Faversham, Kent. *1, 8.*

BARKER, Theodore Cardwell, M.A., Ph.D., University Professor. **MANCHESTER,** Lancashire, 19 July 1923. Publications include: "A Merseyside Town in the Industrial Revolution" (with J. R. Harris), "The Girdlers' Company", "Pilkington Brothers and the Glass Industry", "A History of London Transport" (vol. 1.), (with R. M. Robbins), "The Carpenters Company" (with B. W. E. Alford), etc. Minsen Dane, Faversham, Kent. *8, 9, 35.*

BARKER, W(illiam) A(lan), M.A.(Cantab.), M.A.(Yale), Headmaster. **EDINBURGH,** Scotland, 1 October 1923. *Awarded Harkness Fellowship; Formerly Fellow of Queen's College, Cambridge.* Author of "A General History of England, 1688–1960" (2 vols.), "The Civil War in America". Luckboat House, King Street, Sandwich, Kent. *1, 2, 8, 9, 10, 63.*

BATCHELOR, Paula Vivien, College Tutor. **LONDON.** Publications include: "Bed Majestical", "Angel with Bright Hair". 2a Douglas Road, Maidstone, Kent. *8, 9.*

BATES, Herbert Ernest, C.B.E., Author. Born 16 May 1905. Former Squadron Leader, R.A.F. Author of many publications, including: "The Two Sisters", "Catherine Foster", "Charlotte's Row", "The Fallow Land", "The Poacher", "A House of Women", "Spella Ho", "Fair Stood the Wind for France", "The Purple Plain", "The Jacaranda Tree", "Dear Life", "The Scarlet Sword", "Love for Lydia", "The Feast of July", "The Sleepless Moon", "The Darling Buds of May", "When the Green Woods Laugh", "The Day of the Tortoise", "A Crown of Wild Myrtle", "Oh! To Be In England", "A Moment of Time", "The Distant Horns of Summer", "The Wild Cherry-Tree" ,"The Triple Echo"; several volumes of short stories; "The Vanished World" (autobiography), "The Blossoming World" (autobiography), "Flowers and Faces", "Through the Woods", "Down the River", "The Seasons and the Gardener", "The Last Bread", "The Modern Short Story", "The Heart of the Country", "The Country of White Clover", "A Love of Flowers", etc. The Granary, Little Chart, Kent. *1, 8.*

BEATY, (Arthur) David, M.A.(Oxon), Civil Servant, **HATTON,** Ceylon, 28 March 1919. (*pseud.* Paul Stanton) *Aero Club of France Literature Nomination (1960).* Publications include: "The Heart of the Storm", "The Proving Flight", "Cone of Silence", "The Wind Off the Sea", "The Siren Song", "The Human Factor in Aircraft Accidents", "The Temple Tree", etc. Woodside, Hever, Edenbrdge, Kent. *8.*

BECKETT, Arnold Heyworth, D.Sc., Ph.D., F.R.I.C., F.P.S., University Professor. **BLACKPOOL,** Lancashire, 12 February 1920. Lynwood, Southill Road, Chislehurst, Kent. *1, 8, 35.*

BEHA, Ernest Andrew, Editor. **LONDON,** 1908. Publications include: "Dictionary of Freemasonry", etc. 11a Calverley Park Crescent, Tunbridge Wells, Kent. *8.*

BENEMY, Frank William Georgeson, B.Sc.(Econ.)(London), M.A., Schoolmaster. **RANGOON,** Burma, 1909. *General Secretary, Politics Association, since 1969; Member, Schools Council Social Sciences Committee, since 1967, etc.* Publications include: "Whitehall-Townhall", "Industry Income and Investment", "The Queen Reigns", "The Elected Monarch", "Constitutional Government and West Africa", etc. 10 Holmdene Close, Beckenham, Kent BR3 1AL. *8.*

BENTON, K(enneth) C(arter), C.M.G., B.A.(London), Diplomatic Service (retired). **SUTTON COLDFIELD,** Warwickshire, 4 March 1909. *Committee Member, Crime Writers' Association.* Publications include: "Twenty-fourth Level", "Sole Agent", "Spy in Chancery", etc. Vine House, Appledore, Ashford, Kent. *1, 8, 9, 30, 32.*

BENTON, Peggie, F.I.L., Writer. **VALLETTA,** Malta, 19 October 1916. (*pseud.* Shifty Burke.) *Recipient of Bronze Medal, International Cookery Exhibition, Darmstadt (1964); Bronze Medal, Frankfurt Book Fair (1968).* Publications include: "Peterman", "One Man Against the Drylands", "Finnish Food", etc. Vine House, Appledore, Ashford, Kent. *8, 9.*

BEWES, Canon Thomas Francis Cecil, M.A., Clergyman. Author of "Kikuyu Conflict". The Vicarage, Tonbridge, Kent. *15.*

BILAINKIN, George, Diplomatic Correspondent, Author and Lecturer. Born 12 February 1903. Publications include: "Lim Seng Hooi", "Hail Penang", "Within Two Years", "Front Page News Once", "Changing Opinions", "Poland's Destiny", "Diary of a Diplomatic Correspondent", "Maisky" (biography), "Second Diary of a Diplomatic Correspondent", "Four Weeks in Yugoslavia", "Tito" (biography), "Cairo to Riyadh Diary", "Destination Tokyo", "Four Guilty Britons", "Joseph Kennedy's Fateful Embassy", etc. 12 Regency Close, Sheerness, Kent. *1, 8.*

BINGLEY, D(avid) E(rnest), Teacher. **HUNSLET,** Leeds, Yorkshire, 16 April 1920. (*pseuds.* Henry Chesham, David Horsley.) This author has twenty-eight other pseudonyms mainly used for novels. *Thrice Committee member of the Writers' Summer School at the Hayes, Swanwick, Derbyshire.* 9 Millfields Road, Hythe, Kent. *10.*

BLAXLAND, Pamela C(live) M(ary), J.P., Housewife. **LONDON,** 20 October 1921. (*pseud.* Pamela Luson.) Publications include: "Julia". Waterways, Temple Ewell, Dover, Kent.

BLAXLAND, (William) Gregory, Writer. **NORWICH,** Norfolk, 7 December 1918. Publications include: "J. H. Thomas: A Life for Unity", "Objective Egypt", "The Farewell Years: The Buffs 1948–67", "Amiens 1918", "The Regiments Depart: A History of the British Army, 1945–70", "The Buffs" (Famous Regiment Series), "Golden Miller", etc. Lower Heppington, Street End, Canterbury, Kent. *8, 9.*

BOOTH, Arthur Harold, Journalist. **BIRMINGHAM,** Warwickshire, 1902. Publications include: "British Hustings (1924–50)", "The True Book About Sir Winston Churchill", "The True Book About the First World War", "The True Book About The French Revolution", "The True Book About the Great Religions", "The True Book About Queen Victoria", "The True Book About the American Civil War", "The True Book About Sir Christopher Wren", "William Henry Fox Talbot", etc. 10 Rafford Way, Bromley, Kent. *8.*

BOURDEAUX, Michael Alan, M.A.(Hons.), B.D.(Oxon.), Research Fellow, Royal Institute of International Affairs. **PRAZE,** Cornwall, 19 March 1934. *British Council Exchange Scholar to U.S.S.R., 1959–1960; Anglo-Israel Association Scholar (Wyndham-Deedes) to Israel, 1964; "Crusade" Book Club Author of the Month, January, 1971.* Publications include: "Opium of the People", "Religious Ferment in Russia", "Patriarch and Prophets", "Faith on Trial in Russia", etc. 34 Lubbock Road, Chislehurst, Kent BR7 5JJ. *8, 9, 10.*

BOURQUIN, Paul (Henry) (James), A.I.L., Schoolmaster. **LONDON,** 7 January 1916. (*pseud.* Richard Amberley.) Publications include: "The Lord of the Ravens", "Beltane Fires", "The Cockpit", "The Seven Reductions", "The Land of Delight", "Incitement to Murder", "Phocas the Gardener", "Death on the Stone", "An Ordinary Accident", etc. c/o Winant, Towers Ltd., 1 Furnival Street, London EC4. *This author resides in Kent. 8.*

BRADE-BIRKS, Rev. Canon S(tanley) Graham, M.Sc.(Manchester), D.Sc.(London), F.S.A., Hon.F.L.S., F.Z.S., Clerk in Holy Orders. **BURNAGE,** Lancashire, 2 November 1887. Publications include: "Good Soil", "Teach Yourself Archaeology", etc. Godmersham Vicarage, Canterbury, Kent. *8, 9, 15, 35.*

BRANDON, Owen (Rupert), M.A.(Bristol), M.Litt.(Durham), A.B.Ps.S., A.L.C.D., Minister of Religion. **LONDON,** 24 January 1908. Publications include: "The Battle for the Soul", "Christianity from Within", "The Pastor and his Ministry", etc. Fordwich Rectory, Canterbury, Kent. *8, 15.*

BRANGHAM, Arthur Norman, Writer and Editor. **LONDON,** 6 March 1916. Re-write editor of "The Companion Guide to the South of France" (by Archibald Lyall). Author of "The Naturalist's Riviera", etc. 85 Claremont Road, Tunbridge Wells, Kent.

BRASHER, N(orman) H(enry), M.A.(Cantab.), Schoolmaster. **CHELTENHAM,** Gloucestershire, 16 June 1922. Publications include: "Studies in British Government", "Britain in the 20th Century: 1900–1966" (with E. E. Reynolds), "Arguments in History: Britain in the 19th Century", "The Young Historian", etc. 79 Goddington Lane, Orpington, Kent BR6 9DT. *8, 10.*

BROOKS, Kathleen Ida, Dip.C.D., Teacher. **BARROW-IN-FURNESS,** Lancashire. Publications include: "Play and Learn" (4 books), "Play with Numbers" (2 books), "Man in the Desert", "Man Grows Fruit", "First Steps in Reading" (4 Books), "Reading a Contour Map", etc. 7 Ersham Road, Canterbury, Kent. *8, 35.*

BROUGHTON, Geoffrey, B.A.(Hons.), M.Phil.(London), A.C.P., F.R.S.A., University Lecturer. **NAVENBY,** Lincolnshire, 2 March 1927. Publications include: "Success with English", etc. 3 The Avenue, Beckenham, Kent. *8.*

BROWN, Rev. David (Alan), B.A., B.D., M.Th., A.L.C.D., Minister of Religion. **BRISTOL,** Gloucestershire, 11 July 1922. Publications include: "The Way of the Prophet", "Preaching Patterns", "Jesus and God", "The Christian Scriptures", "The Cross of the Messiah", "The Divine Trinity", "Evangelism is Living", etc. The Vicarage, Charles Street, Herne Bay, Kent. *15.*

BRUFORD, Rose (Elizabeth), Hon.R.A.M., Founder College of Speech and Drama. **LONDON,** 22 June 1904. *Founder and Principal, Rose Bruford College of Speech and Drama (1950–1967); Hon. Member, Guild of Drama Adjudicators, and Society of Teachers of Speech and Drama, etc.* Publications include: "Speech and Drama", "Teaching Mime", etc. Old Kennels House, Otford, near Sevenoaks, Kent. *1, 8, 14, 53.*

BULL, Guyon Boys Garrett, M.A.(Cantab.), Ph.D.(London), University (College) Departmental Head. **KINGSCLERE,** Berkshire, 1912. Publications include: "North America", "A Town Study Companion", etc. Loring Hall, North Cray, Sidcup, Kent. *8, 9.*

BULMER, H(enry) K(enneth), Author. **LONDON,** 1921. Publications include: "The Doomsday Men", "The Ulcer Culture", "City under the Sea", "To Outrun Doomsday", "Pretenders", "Roller-Coaster World", " Kandar", etc. 19 Orchard Way, Horsmonden, Kent. *8, 9, 10.*

BUNCH, Rev. Francis Christopher, M.A., Clergyman. Joint author of "Prayers at Home", "Prayers at School". Otford Vicarage, Sevenoaks, Kent. *15.*

BURGEON, G. A. L. *see* BARFIELD, (Arthur) Owen.

BURKE, Shifty *see* BENTON, Peggie.

CARLEY, James, F.C.A., Chartered Accountant. **LEYTON,** Essex, 2 October 1913. Publications include: "The Lost Roads of Meopham", "Public Transport Timetables 1838". 48 Windmill Street, Gravesend, Kent.

CARTER, Cedric Oswald, M.A., D.M.(Oxon.), F.R.C.P., Medical Geneticist. Born 26 September 1917. Publications include: "Human Heredity", "A.B.C. of Medical Genetics", etc. Holly Lodge, 42 Forest Drive, Keston Park, Keston, Kent BR2 6EF. *8, 9.*

CHACE, Isobel *see* HUNTER, Elizabeth (Mary) (Teresa).

CHESHAM, Henry *see* BINGLEY, D(avid) E(rnest).

CHILDE, Henry Langdon, Editor (retired). **LONDON,** 1892. Author of "Concrete Products and Cast Stone", "Precast Concrete Factory Operation", "Introduction to Concrete Work", "Everyman's Guide to Concrete Work", "Concrete Roofing Tiles", "Concrete Surface Finishes", "Practical Concrete Work", "Concrete Finishes and Decoration", etc. 20 Uplands Way, Sevenoaks, Kent. *8.*

CHILSTON, Viscount (Eric Alexander Akers-Douglas). **VIENNA,** Austria, 17 December 1910. Publications include: "Chief Whip: The Political Life and Times of A. Akers-Douglas, 1st Viscount Chilston"; "W. H. Smith"; part author "Survey of International Affairs", 1938–1948, etc. Chilston Park, Sandway, near Maidstone, Kent. *1, 7, 32.*

CHILTON, Charles Frederick William, Script Writer, TV and Radio Producer. **LONDON,** 1917. Publications include: "Journey into Space," "The Red Planet", "The World in Peril", "Square Dance Manual", "Boys' Book of the West", "Encyclopaedia of the West", "Riders of the Range" (annual), etc. 27 Commonside, Keston, Kent. *8.*

CHISHOLM, Lilian, Novelist. **LONDON,** 28 March 1906. (*pseud.* Anne Lorraine.) Author of approximately 100 romances. 37 The Knoll, Hayes, Kent.　*8.*

CLARK, Lord (Kenneth Mackenzie), C.H., K.C.B., F.B.A., Chancellor of the University of York. **LONDON,** 13 July 1903. *Recipient of numerous honorary, doctorates and several overseas decorations.* Publications include: "The Gothic Revival", "Commemorative Catalogue of Exhibition of Italian Art", "Catalogue of Drawings of Leonardo da Vinci in the collection of His Majesty the King at Windsor Castle" (part author and editor), "One Hundred Details in the National Gallery", "Leonardo da Vinci", "Last Lectures by Roger Fry" (edited), "L. B. Alberti on Painting", "Constable's Hay Wain", "Landscape into Art", "Piero della Francesca", "Moments of Vision", "The Nude", "Looking", "Ruskin Today", "Rembrandt and the Italian Renaissance", "A Failure of Nerve", "Civilisation", etc. Saltwood Castle, Kent.　*1, 8, 9, 31, 32.*

CLARK, Gerald Roy. **NORWICH,** Norfolk, 1911. *Editor, BBC Magazine Programme, 1953–1960; Founder, Norfolk Wherry Trust, 1949.* Author of "Black-Sailed Traders", etc. 23 North Down Close, Maidstone, Kent.　*8.*

CLARK, S(tanley) C(harles), M.A.(Cantab.), Clerk in Holy Orders. **ALDERSHOT,** Hampshire, 1 March 1929. Publications include: "Unity, Uniformity, and the English Church", "The Second Advent". The Vicarage, Crockenhill, Swanley, Kent BR8 8JY.　*15.*

CODRINGTON, K(enneth) de B(urgh), M.A., University Professor (Emeritus). **MURREE,** India, 5 June 1899. Publications include: "Ancient India", "An Introduction to the Study of Medieval Indian Sculpture", "An Introduction to the Study of Islamic Art in India", "The Wood of the Image", "Cricket in the Grass", "Birdwood and the Arts of India", etc. Rose Cottage, Appledore, Kent.　*1, 7, 8, 9.*

COLE, C(hristopher) C(harles) H(arry), Senior Information Officer, Ministry of Defence (Royal Air Force Public Relations). **TODDING-TON,** Bedfordshire, 2 November 1916. Publications include: "McCudden VC", "Royal Air Force 1918" (editor), "Royal Flying Corps 1915–1918" (editor). Chance Cottage, Seal Chart, Sevenoaks, **Kent.**　*8.*

COLQUHOUN, Rev. Canon Frank, M.A., Clergyman. **VENTNOR,** Isle of Wight, 28 October 1909. Publications include: "Harringay Story", "The Gospels", "Total Christianity", "The Catechism", "Parish Prayers", etc. 77 Rectory Road, Beckenham, Kent BR3 1HR. *1, 8, 9, 15.*

COOK, Charles Thomas, D.D., Baptist Pastor and Editor. **LONDON,** 1886. Publications include: "Behold the Throne of Grace", "The Billy Graham Story", "London Hears Billy Graham", "Tell Me About Moody", etc. 14 Church Road, Shortlands, Kent. *8.*

COOPER, Bryan, Writer. **PARIS,** France, 6 February 1932. Publications include: "North Sea Oil—The Great Gamble", "The Ironclads of Cambrai", "Battle of the Torpedo Boats", "The Buccaneers", "Alaska—The Last Frontier", etc. Hurst Farm House, Weald, near Sevenoaks, Kent. *8, 10.*

COPPER, Basil, Author. **LONDON,** 1924. *Member, Committee of Crime Writers' Association.* Publications include: "The Dark Mirror", "Night Frost", "No Flowers for the General", "Scratch on the Dark", "Not After Nightfall", "Die Now, Live Later", "Don't Bleed On Me", "The Marble Orchard", "Dead File", "No Letters from the Grave", "The Big Chill", "Flash-Point", "The Vampire: in Legend, Fact and Art", "From Evil's Pillow", etc. Stockdoves, South Park, Sevenoaks, Kent. *8, 9.*

CORBETT, John A., B.A., Ph.D., Director of Education. **WADSLEY BRIDGE,** Yorkshire, 4 May 1908. High Halden, Kent. *9, 58.*

COWELL, Frank Richard, C.M.G., B.A., B.Sc.(Econ.), Ph.D.(London), retired Civil Servant. **LONDON,** 16 November 1897. Publications include: "Brief Guide to Government Publications", "Cicero and the Roman Republic", "History, Civilization and Culture", "Culture", "Everyday Life in Ancient Rome", "Revolutions in Ancient Rome", "Values in Human Society", "The Dominance of Rome", etc. Crowdleham House, Kemsing, Kent. *1, 8, 9.*

COX, Rev. David, M.A., B.D., Clergyman. Author of "Jung and St. Paul", "History and Myth", "What Christians Believe", "How the Mind Works". All Saints' Vicarage, Maidstone Road, Chatham, Kent. *15.*

CRAGG, Rt. Rev. (Albert) Kenneth, D.Phil., Assistant Bishop to the Archbishop in Jerusalem. Born 8 March 1913. Publications include: "The Call of the Minaret", "Sandals at the Mosque", "The Dome and the Rock", "Counsels in Contemporary Islam", "Christianity in World Perspective", "The Privilege of Man", "The House of Islam", "Alive to God", "The Event of the Qur'an", "The Theology of Unity", etc. 59 Prospect Road, Southborough, Tunbridge Wells, Kent.   *1, 15.*

CRAGG, Ven. Herbert Wallace, M.A., Archdeacon of Bromley. Born 18 November 1910. Publications include: "The Sole Sufficiency of Jesus Christ", "The Holy Spirit and the Christian Life", "The Encouragement of the Believer", "Victory in the Christian Life". Christ Church Vicarage, 61 Hayes Lane, Beckenham, Kent BR3 2RE. *1, 15.*

CROOK, Herbert Clifford. **EASTBOURNE,** Sussex, 1882. *Vice-President, Alpine Garden Society.* Author of "Campanulas", "Campanulas and Bellflowers in Cultivation", etc. 4 Alexandra Crescent, Bromley, Kent.   *8.*

CROUCH, Marcus, B.A.(London), F.L.A., Librarian, **TOTTENHAM,** Middlesex, 12 February 1913. Publications include: "Treasure Seekers and Borrowers", "Kent", "Essex", "Heritage of Sussex", "Canterbury". Springfield, Maidstone, Kent.   *8, 9.*

CROWTHER, Doreen Stoddart, Writer on Horticulture and Editor. *Assistant Editor of "Amateur Gardening", 1947–1953.* 22 Bromley Common, Bromley, Kent.   *9.*

CRUICKSHANK, Alexander, O.B.E., M.D.(Aberdeen). **ABERDEEN,** Scotland, 1900. Author of "The Kindling Fire", etc. Cranmers, Worships Hill, Riverhead, Kent.   *8, 63.*

CUMMINGS, Richard Gordon, Public Relations Adviser. Writer on finance and economics. The Gatehouse, The Green, Frant, Tunbridge Wells, Kent.   *9.*

CURTEIS, Ian (Bayley), Playwright. **LONDON,** 1 May 1935. Publications include: "Long Voyage Out of War". Little Hatch, Mersham, near Ashford, Kent.   *8, 9, 70.*

CURTIS, Tom *see* PENDOWER, Jacques.

DALE, Doreen Stoddart *see* CROWTHER, Doreen Stoddart.

DALZELL-WARD, Arthur James, M.R.C.S., L.R.C.P., D,P.H., F.R.S.H., Medical Officer and Lecturer. **GUILDFORD,** Surrey, 1914. Joint author of "Text Book of Health Education", etc. Green Shutters, 631 Hurst Road, Bexley, Kent. *8.*

DANBY, Hope. **SYDNEY,** Australia, 21 March 1899. Author of "The Illustrious Emperor", "The Garden of Perfect Brightness", "My Boy Chang". The White Cottage, Sandhurst, Kent. *8, 9.*

DAVIDSON, Rev. Isaac Emmanuel, Clergyman. Author of "The Feast of the Passover", "These Things", "The Tabernacle—Its Symbolism", "The Atonement", "Readings in Revelation". 35 Woodride, Petts Wood, Orpington, Kent. *15.*

DAVIS, Alec, Company Director, Editor and Typographer. **BOSTON,** Lincolnshire, 1912. Publications include: "Type in Advertising", "Package and Print", etc. 47 Links Way, Beckenham, Kent BR3 3DG. *8.*

DAVIS, Dennis J., **LONDON,** 1933. Publications include: "The Book of Canoeing", "The Thames Sailing Barge", etc. 12 Cecil Park, Herne Bay, Kent. *8.*

DEACON, Richard *see* McCORMICK, (George) Donald (King).

DEMPSTER, Derek David, M.A.(Cantab.). **TANGIER,** Morocco, 1924. Publications include: "The Inhabited Universe" (with K. Gatland), "The Tale of the Comet", "The Narrow Margin" (with D. H. Wood), etc. Upton House, Worth, near Sandwich, Kent. *8.*

DOBSON, Kenneth Austin, B.A.(Oxon.), **SHANGHAI,** China, 1907. Author of "Mail Train", "The Inescapable Wilderness", "District Commissioner", "Colour Blind", etc. Priors, Jackass Lane, Keston, Kent BR2 6AN. *8.*

DOWER, Penn *see* PENDOWER, Jacques.

DRIVER, C(harles) J(onathan), B.A.(Hons.), B.Ed., S.T.D.(Cape Town), B.Phil.(Oxon.), Schoolmaster. **CAPE TOWN,** South Africa, 19 August 1939. Author of "Elegy for a Revolutionary", "Send War in Our Time, O Lord", "Death of Fathers", etc. International Centre, Sevenoaks School, Oak Lane, Sevenoaks, Kent. *8, 9, 10, 12.*

DRUMMOND, John Dorman, Editor. **GLASGOW,** Scotland, 1915. Author of "Through Hell and High Water", "Seagulls Over Sorrento", "H.M. U-Boat", "A River Runs To War", "Blue For a Girl", "The Story of the W.R.N.S.", "But For These Men", "Gaps of Danger", etc. 15 The Avenue, Beckenham, Kent. *8, 63.*

DUNCAN, Kathleen Mary. **ENFIELD,** Middlesex, 1907. (*pseuds.* Catherine Simmons, Kim Simmons.) Publications include: "Secrets at Saxonhill", "Crispins Castle", "No Dogs Allowed", "Caravan Stowaways", "Keren's Secret Room", etc. Seaward Cottage, 25 Devonshire Road, Dover, Kent. *8.*

DUNSTONE, Max(well) (Frederick), Customs Officer (retired). **LONDON,** 1915. Author of "Cornet of Dragoons", "The Customs Officer", etc. 1 Cordova Court, Sandgate Road, Folkestone, Kent. *8.*

DURANT, G(ladys) M(ay), B.A.(London), Grammar School Teacher (retired). **PRITTLEWELL,** Southend-on-Sea, Essex, 13 September 1899. Author of "Journey into Roman Britain", "Discovering Medieval Art", "Britain: Rome's Most Northerly Province", "Landscape with Churches", etc. Flat 2, 30 Kingsnorth Gardens, Folkestone, Kent. *8, 9.*

EARLE, Rev. Nicholas Albert Edward, M.A., LL.B., Clergyman. Author of "The Coming Kingdom and the Coming King". 30 Molyneux Park Road, Tunbridge Wells, Kent. *15.*

EDMISTON, (Helen) Jean (Mary), B.A.(London), Assistant Editor, Journal of Medical Research. **SOUTHPORT,** Lancashire, 9 August 1913. (*pseud.* Helen Robertson.) Author of "The Winged Witnesses", "Venice of the Black Sea", "The Shake-Up", "The Crystal-gazers", "The Chinese Goose", etc. 77 Knockhall Chase, Greenhithe, Kent. *8, 35.*

EDMONDS, C(ecil) J(ohn), C.M.G., C.B.E., Minister in H.M. Foreign Service (retired). **OSAKA,** Japan 26 October 1889. *Awarded: Order of the (Iraq) Rafidain (Class II), 1945; Burton Memorial Medal (Royal Asiatic Society), 1963; Sykes Memorial Medal (Royal Central Asian Society), 1966. Vice-President (1949–1953, 1959–1962), Royal Central Asian Society; Vice-President, British School of Archaeology in Iraq.* Publications include: "Kurds, Turks and Arabs", "A Pilgrimage to Lalish", "A Kurdish-English Dictionary", (joint), etc. 5 Longslip, Langton Green, Tunbridge Wells, Kent. *1, 6, 7, 8, 10, 30.*

EDMONDS, Harry, Company Director. **MERTHYR TYDFIL,** Glamorgan, Wales, 1891. Author of "North Sea Mystery", "Red Desert", "Riddle of Straits", "Red Invader", "Trail of the Lonely River", "East Coast Mystery", "Wind in the East", "Across the Frontiers", "The Orphans of Brandenburg", "A British Five-Year Plan", "Yvonne", "The Death Ship", "Professor's Last Experiment", "Home to Southey", "The Secret Voyage", "The Clockmaker of Heidelberg", "The Rockets", etc. 1 Brockhill Road, Hythe, Kent. *8, 62.*

EDMONDSON, Sybil, Writer. **LONDON,** 1898. (*pseud.* Sybil Armstrong.) Author of "No Sluggard in Arcadia", "Myrtle and Anne", etc. Sealawn, 43 Joy Lane, Whitstable, Kent. *8.*

ELLINGHAM, Rev. Cecil John, M.A., Clergyman. Joint editor of "Greece and Rome". Somerden, Groombridge, Tunbridge Wells, Kent. *15.*

EYRE, Annette *see* WORBOYS, Annette Isobel.

FAINLIGHT, Ruth (Esther) (Mrs. Alan Sillitoe), Writer. **NEW YORK CITY,** U.S.A. 2 May 1931. Publications include: "Cages" (poems), "To See The Matter Clearly" (poems), "Daylife and Nightlife" (stories), etc. 21 The Street, Wittersham, Kent. *9, 11, 12.*

FARRELL, Alan (John Joseph), M.A.(Oxon.), Schoolmaster. **RAINFORD,** Lancashire, 1920. Author of "Sir Winston Churchill". 29 Harvest Bank Road, West Wickham, Kent BR4 9DL. *8, 9, 35.*

FINLAY, John Alexander Robertson, M.A.(Glasgow and Oxford), **BELHEVIE,** Aberdeenshire, Scotland, 1917. Author of "The Trustees' Handbook", "The Landlord and Tenant Act", etc. Thornhill, Golf Road, Bickley, Kent. *8, 63.*

FLOWERDEW, Phyllis *see* KINGSBURY, Phyllis (May).

FOSTER, George *see* HASWELL, Chetwynd John Drake.

FOX, Ronald William, Teacher. **LONDON,** 1921. Publications include: "Certificate Mathematics 1, 2, 3", "Mathematical Tables and Data" (co-author), etc. Honeymede, 16 Wivenhoe Close, Rainham, Kent. *8.*

FOXELL, Rev. Maurice, K.C.V.O., M.A., Extra Chaplain to the Queen. Born 15 August 1888. Author of "Wren's Craftsmen at St. Paul's Cathedral". Jay Cottage, Lamberhurst, Kent. *1, 15.*

FRASER, Edith, Teacher. **FRIERN BARNET,** Middlesex, 14 January 1903. Publications include: "The Voyage to There and Back", "David John" (Book of the Month Choice, *News Chronicle,* September 1958), "The Bible Tells Me So", "David John Hears About Jesus", "David John Again", "Before Jesus Came", "David John Finds Out", "Nelson's New Job", "The Shining Star", "The Prodigal Son", "The Little Boat", etc. Grunnavoe, 1 Admiralty Walk, Whitstable, Kent. *8, 9, 10.*

FREEMAN, Dave *see* FREEMAN, David.

FREEMAN, David, Writer, specialising in TV comedy scripts. **LONDON,** 1922. Pedlars Farm, Biddenden, Kent.   *8.*

FREESTONE, Basil. **HAMPTON WICK,** Middlesex, 1910. Author of "Golden Drum", "Crave Pity from the Wind", "Pegasus Book of Good English", "The Sea is Not Full", etc. 72 Borstal Road, Rochester, Kent.   *8.*

FROST, Rex, M.H.C.I. **LONDON,** 1914. Author of "Small Hotel", "The Travellers", etc. The Lodge, Boughton Monchelsea Place, near Maidstone, Kent.   *8.*

FULLERTON, Alexander Fergus, Novelist. **SAXMUNDHAM,** Suffolk, 1924. Author of "Surface", "Bury the Past", "No Man's Mistress", "A Wren Called Smith", "The White Men Sang", "The Yellow Ford", "The Waiting Game", "Soldier from the Sea", "The Thunder and the Flame", "Lionheart", "Chief Executive", "The Publisher", etc. Little Farnham, Langton Green, near Tunbridge Wells, Kent. *8, 9.*

GARRETT, Richard, Journalist. **LONDON,** 15 January 1920. *Fellow, British Association of Industrial Editors.* Publications include: "Fast and Furious", "The Motor Racing Story", "The Rally-Go-Round", "Anatomy of a Grand Prix Driver", "Great Sea Mysteries", "Atlantic Jet", "Motoring and the Mighty", "Hoaxes and Swindles", "Cross-Channel and True Tales of Detection", etc. Oak Cottage, 41 Warwick Park, Tunbridge Wells, Kent.

GIBSON, James Charles, M.A.(Cantab.), Principal Lecturer in English, Christ Church College, Canterbury. **WANDSWORTH,** London, 1919. Publications include: "Evelyn and Pepys", "Reading Aloud", "Solo and Chorus", "Rhyme and Rhythm", "Poetry and Song", "As Large as Alone", etc. 26 St. Lawrence Forstal, Canterbury, Kent. *8.*

GILBERT, Michael Francis, LL.B.(London). **BILLINGHAY,** Lincolnshire, 1912. Author of twelve novels of detection; editor of "Crime in Good Company", etc. Luddesdown Old Rectory, Gravesend, Kent. *8.*

GLENCROSS, Alan. **WARRINGTON,** Lancashire, 17 December 1920. Renhold, London Road, Dunton Green, Sevenoaks, Kent. *35.*

GODDARD, Air Marshal Sir (Robert) Victor, K.C.B., C.B.E., M.A. (Cantab.). Born 1897. Author of "The Enigma of Menace". Meadowgate, Brasted, near Westerham, Kent. *1, 8, 32.*

GODDEN, Jon, Novelist. **MIDNAPUR,** Bengal, India, 3 August 1906. Author of nine novels, including: "The House by the Sea", "The Peacock", "The City and the Wave", "The Seven Islands", "Mrs. Panopoulis", "In the Sun", "Kitten with Blue Eyes", etc. Lydd House, Aldington, near Ashford, Kent. *8, 9.*

GODFREY, Ernest Gordon, M.C., Author and Editor. **MIDDLESEX,** 1897. Sometime Editor of "Contemporary Review", etc. Publications include: "Cast-Iron Sixth", "Serial Maps" (with Goodall), "Ports, Dues and Charges on Shipping" (with K. MacDonald), "The Duke of Cornwall's Light Infantry, 1939–1945" (with Major-General R. F. K. Goldsmith), etc. Old Mead Farm, Marshside, Canterbury, Kent. *8.*

GODMAN, Arthur, B.Sc., A.R.I.C., Dip.Ed. **HEREFORD,** 1916. Publications include: "Every Day Science for the Tropics", "Health Science for the Tropics", "Upper Primary Arithmetic", "Every Day Science for Malaysia", "Malaysian General Mathematics", "Remove Mathematics", "General Science Certificate Course", "Practical Certificate Chemistry", "Chemistry, A New Certificate Approach", "Junior Tropical Biology", etc. Sondes House, Patrixbourne, Canterbury, Kent. *8.*

GOODRIDGE, Rev. Frank, A.K.C., Clergyman. Editor of The Language of the Silent World". 185 Farnaby Road, Bromley, Kent BR2 0BA. *15.*

GOODSALL, Robert H(arold), F.R.I.B.A., F.R.P.S., F.S.A., Architect, Farmer and Estate Owner. **STREATHAM,** London, 17 October 1891. Publications include: "Home Building", "Palestine Memories"; "Whitstable, Seasalter and Swalecliffe", "Stede Hill", "The Kentish Stour", "The Medway and its Tributaries", "The Ancient Road to Canterbury", "The Eastern Rother", "The Arun and Western Rother", "The Widening Thames", "A Kentish Patchwork", "A Second Kentish Patchwork", "A Third Kentish Patchwork", etc. Stede Hill, Harrietsham, near Maidstone, Kent.   *8, 9.*

GRAEME, Bruce *see* JEFFRIES, Graham Montague.

GRAEME, Roderic *see* JEFFRIES, Roderic (Graeme).

GRAY, Canon George Harold Magrath, M.A., Clergyman. Author of "The Meaning of the Gospel". Roxburgh House, Cranbrook, Kent. *15.*

GREEN, Thomas Michael Ramsay, Editor. **HALIFAX,** Yorkshire. Publications include: "Unconsidered Trifles", "From a Pennine Window", etc. Beechcroft, Park Road, Southborough, Tunbridge Wells, Kent.   *8, 58.*

GREEN, William, Consultant Editor. **LONDON,** 1927. Publications include: "The Air Forces of the World", "The Observer's Book of Aircraft", "The Observer's World Aircraft Directory", "The Aircraft of the World", "The Jet Aircraft of the World", "Famous Fighters of the Second World War", "Famous Bombers of the Second World War", "The World's Fighting Planes", etc. High Timber, Chislehurst Road, Chislehurst, Kent.   *8.*

GREGOR, Ian, B.A., Ph.D., Professor of Modern English Literature. **NEWCASTLE UPON TYNE,** Northumberland, 1926. Publications include: "The Moral and The Story" (with Brian Nicholas), "William Golding" (with Mark Kinkead-Weekes), "Matthew Arnold, Culture and Anarchy" (editor), etc. Rutherford College, University of Kent, Canterbury, Kent.   *8.*

GREGORY, James Stothert, B.A.(London), F.R.G.S., Senior Lecturer in Geography, Furzedown College of Education. **MANCHESTER,** Lancashire, 1912. Publications include: "The USSR: a Geographical Survey", "Land of the Soviets", "Atlas of USSR" (with V. H. Horrabin), "Malayan Primary Geography" (Series), "Russian Land, Soviet People", etc. 167 High Street, Queenborough, Isle of Sheppey, Kent.   *8, 35.*

GRENVILLE-MALET, Baldwyn Hugh, M.A.(Cantab.), Author, and Director of Studies, Brasted Theological Training College. **SALISBURY,** Wiltshire, 13 February 1928. (*pseud.* Hugh Malet.) Publications include: "Voyage in a Bowler Hat", "The Canal Duke", "In the Wake of the Gods", etc. Brasted Place College, near Westerham, Kent. *8, 10, 14.*

HALLS, Hamish, M.A., Art Historian, and Lecturer, Canterbury College of Art. **NORTH QUEENSFERRY,** Fife, Scotland, 27 May 1942. *Diploma in History of Art (Courtauld Institute).* Author of "Canterbury" (in Studio Vista *City Buildings* Series). c/o Canterbury College of Art, New Dover Road, Canterbury, Kent.

HARDINGE OF PENSHURST, Lady Helen, Writer. **LONDON,** 11 May 1901. Author of "The Path of Kings", "Loyal to Three Kings", etc. South Park, Penshurst, Tonbridge, Kent.

HARDWICK, Mary Elizabeth, M.A.(Cantab.), Headmistress of Bromley High School. **MANSFIELD,** Nottinghamshire, 1925. Author of "Brevitas: a text book of Latin constructions". 14a Highfield Road, Bickley, Kent. *8.*

HARDWICK, Michael, F.R.S.A., Author, Playwright and Producer of Radio Drama. **LEEDS,** Yorkshire, 10 September 1924. *Member of Council, Sherlock Holmes Society of London.* Publications (many with Mollie Hardwick) include: "The Sherlock Holmes Companion", "The Man Who Was Sherlock Holmes", "Four Sherlock Holmes Plays", "The Charles Dickens Companion", "The Game's Afoot—Four More Sherlock Holmes Plays", "The Bernard Shaw Companion", "Writers' Houses", "Alfred Deller: A Singularity of Voice", "Dickens' England", "As They Saw Him: Charles Dickens", "The Charles Dickens Encyclopaedia", "Literary Atlas & Gazetteer of Great Britain", "Companion-Guide to Gilbert & Sullivan", etc. 45 Mount Sion, Tunbridge Wells, Kent. *8, 58.*

HARDWICK, Mollie, F.R.S.A., Author and Journalist. **MANCHESTER,** Lancashire. *Formerly BBC Announcer.* Publications (individually and with Michael Hardwick) include: "The Sherlock Holmes Companion", "The Man who was Sherlock Holmes", "Four Sherlock Holmes Plays", "The Charles Dickens Companion", "Writers' Houses", "Alfred Deller: A Singularity of Voice", "Stories from Dickens", "The Game's Afoot", "Emma, Lady Hamilton", "Dickens's England", "As they Saw Him: Charles Dickens", "Plays From Dickens", etc. 45 Mount Sion, Tunbridge Wells, Kent.   *8, 35.*

HARE, John, M.A.(Oxon.), Dip.Ed.(Reading), Teacher. **HASTINGS,** Sussex, 21 March 1935. *Awarded Bronze Medal, Alliance Francaise (1953), Education Prize, University of Reading (1960). Lecturer and Assistant Professor, Memorial University of Newfoundland (1962-1967), etc.* Author of "The Literature of France". 61 West End, Kemsing, Kent.   *9, 14.*

HARGREAVES, Rev. John Henry Monsarrat, M.A., Clergyman. Author of "A Guide to St. Mark's Gospel", "A Guide to the Parables". St. Luke's Parsonage, Eardley Road, Sevenoaks, Kent. *15.*

HART, Cyril John. **LONDON,** 1919. *Assistant Press Officer, The Royal Society for the Prevention of Accidents, 1955–1960; National Secretary, Speedway Riders' Association, 1959.* Publications include: "True Life Adventure Stories", etc. 77 Perry Hall Road, Orpington, Kent.   *8.*

HART, Harold Eaton, M.C., M.A.(Cantab.), Company Director (retired). **KINGSTON-ON-THAMES,** Surrey, 1893. Author of Several published translations, including: "The Châteaux of France" (by Francois Gebelin), "The Marne" (by Georges Blond), etc. Flat C, 203 Sandgate Road, Folkestone, Kent.   *8.*

HARTCUP, Adeline, M.A.(Oxon.), Author and Journalist, **ISLE OF WIGHT,** 26 April 1918. Author of "Angelica", "Morning Faces". Published translations include: "The Labour and the Wounds", "European Porcelain", "Oriental Carpets", "Villas and Palaces of Europe", etc. Swanton Court, Sevington, Ashford, Kent.   *8, 10.*

HARTCUP, John, Writer. **ELSWICK,** Lancashire, 4 December 1915. Publications include: "Biography of Camille Desmoulins", "Morning Faces", etc. Swanton Court, Sevington, Ashford, Kent.   *8, 10.*

HARTMAN, Henry, Author. **STUTTGART,** Germany, 14 September 1931. (*pseud.* Henry Seymour.) Author of "Intrigue in Tangier", "Run for your Money", "The Bristol Affair", "The Paperchase Murder", "In the Still of the Night", "Apointment with Murder", "Hot Ice", "Infernal Idol", "Cold Wind of Death", etc. 26 Lower Sands Estate, Dymchurch, Kent.   *8.*

HASWELL, Chetwynd John Drake, Author. **PENN,** Buckinghamshire, 18 July 1919. (*pseuds.* Jock Haswell, George Foster.) Author of "Indian File", "Soldier on Loan", "The Queen's Royal Regiment", "The First Respectable Spy", "James II, Soldier and Sailor", "Know Thine Enemy", "Citizen Armies", "The Struggle for Empire", etc. The Grey House, Lyminge, Folkestone, Kent.   *8, 9, 10.*

HASWELL, Jock *see* HASWELL, Chetwynd John Drake.

HATHERLEY, Peter *see* PEAR, T(om) H(atherley).

HATTON, Charles. **STOURBRIDGE,** Worcestershire. Author of "Mr. Everyman", "Alias William Shakespeare", "Maiden Over", "They Can't Hang Me", "Cicero Goes to Brighton", "No Trees in the Street", etc. 12 Crofton Road, Orpington, Kent.   *8.*

HAYES, Juanita, Drama Instructor. Publications include: "The Silver Key", "The King's Daughters", "Standin' in de Need of Pray'r", "Where Angels Fear to Tread", etc. Manor Cottage, Old Road, Elham, near Canterbury, Kent.   *8, 9.*

HEASMAN, Kathleen Joan, M.A.(Cantab.), Ph.D.(London), University Lecturer. **SOUTHSEA,** Hampshire, 24 June 1913. Author of "Evangelicals in Action", "Christians and Social Work", "Army of the Church", "An Introduction to Pastoral Counselling", etc. The White Cottage, Leigh, near Tonbridge, Kent.   *8, 9, 78.*

HEATH, Royton Edward, F.L.S., F.R.I.H.(N.Z.), engaged in Hotel Industry. **DULWICH,** London 7, August 1907. *Awarded gold, silver, and bronze medals during past 25 years for alpine plant culture; recipient of many cultural commendations from the Royal Horticultural Society.* Publications include: "Alpines Under Glass", "Shrubs for Rock Garden", "Miniature Gardening Troughs and Pans", "Collectors Alpines", "Rock Plants for Small Gardens", "Encyclopaedia of Rock Plants", etc. 78 Kingsway, Petts Wood, Orpington, Kent.   *8, 9, 10.*

HEMMING, Commander Jack C(hetwynd) W(estern), R.N.V.R.(retired), F.R.S.A., Writer. **LONDON,** 2 September 1899. (*pseud.* J. C. Western-Holt) Publications include: "Voyage of the Dauntless", "Lost World of the Colorado", "Blue Wings", etc. Cornerways, Riding Lane, Hildenborough, Kent.   *6, 7, 8, 22.*

HETHERINGTON, T(homas) B(aines), M.A., Dip.Ed.(Durham), Academic Registrar and Principal Lecturer in English Literature. **DURHAM CITY,** 7 December 1919. (Writes under "Tom Hetherington.) *Awarded Spence Watson Prize in English Literature (Durham University), 1951.* Publications include: "Across A Still Sleeping World", "The Fighting Man", "The Lion Who Fell", etc. 59 Beaconsfield Road, St. Stephen's, Canterbury, Kent.   *8.*

HICHENS, Jacobine Napier (Lady Sackville), Barrister-at-Law. **GLASGOW,** Scotland, 1920. Author of "Noughts and Crosses", "Touch and Go", "Profit and Loss", etc. Knole, Sevenoaks, Kent. *8, 9.*

HIGENBOTTAM, Frank, B.A., F.L.A., Librarian. Born 25 December 1910. Publications include: "Teach Yourself Concise Encyclopedia of General Knowledge" (with S. G. Brade-Birks), "Teach Yourself Russian through Reading". 17 Glenside Avenue, Canterbury, Kent.

HIGH, Philip E. **BIGGLESWADE,** Bedfordshire, 1914. Author of "Prodigal Son", "No Truce with Terra", "Mad Metropolis", "Reality Forbidden", "Invader on my Back", "These Savage Futurians", "Twin Planets", "The Time Mercenaries", etc. 34 King Street, Canterbury, Kent.   *8.*

HILL, Rev. Canon D(erek) Ingram, M.A.(Oxon), Clerk in Holy Orders. **WIMBLEDON,** London, 11 September 1912. Author of "The Ancient Hospitals and Almshouses of Canterbury", "The Stained Glass of Canterbury Cathedral", etc. The Master's Lodge, Eastbridge Hospital, Canterbury, Kent.   *15.*

HIRST, Alice Elizabeth, M.B.E., M.A.(Leeds), College Teacher (retired). **BAWTRY,** Yorkshire, 1898. Publications include "Benga" (in collaboration with Kamara), "Rassin" (in collaboration with Wurie), etc. The Bungalow, 34 Stanhope Road, Deal, Kent.   *8, 58.*

HOLLAND, Margaret, Writer and Housewife. **MONTCLAIR,** New Jersey, U.S.A., 2 November 1917. Publications include: "Old Country Silver", "English Provincial Silver", etc. The Mast Head, Frant, Tunbridge Wells, Kent.

HOLMAN, Dennis, B.A., Journalist and Author. **LAHORE,** India. Author of "Lady Louis: Life of the Countess Mountbatten of Burma", "Noone of the Ulu", "The Man They Couldn't Kill", "Sikander Sahib", "The Green Torture", "Bwana Drum", "Inside Safari Hunting", "The Elephant People", etc. 48 Christchurch Road, Sidcup, Kent. *8, 9.*

HORSLEY, David *see* BINGLEY, D(avid) E(rnest).

HOUSEHOLD, H(umphrey) G(eorge) W(est), M.A.(Bristol), Schoolmaster, **CHELTENHAM,** Gloucestershire, 5 January 1906. Author of "The Thames and Severn Canal", etc. 1 Marten Road, Folkestone, Kent. *8, 9.*

HOWLETT, John Reginald, B.A.(Oxon.), Author and Scriptwriter. **LEEDS,** Yorkshire, 4 April 1940. Orchard House, Stone in Oxney, Tenterden, Kent. *8, 58.*

HUGHES, G. Bernard, F.R.S.A. **WOLVERHAMPTON,** Staffordshire. Author of "Collecting Antiques", "More About Collecting Antiques", "Horse Brasses & Other Curios", "Victorian Pottery and Porcelain", "Old English, Irish and Scottish Table Glass", "Small Antique Silverware", "English Glass for the Collector", "Three Centuries of English Silver", "Small Antique Furniture", "English Porcelain & Bone China", "Encyclopaedia of English Ceramics", "Old English Pottery", "Three Centuries of English Home Needlework", etc. Fairlight House, Hythe, Kent. *8, 66.*

HUNTER, Elizabeth (Mary) (Teresa), Author. **NAIROBI,** Kenya, 24 October 1934. (*pseud.* Isobel Chace.) Author of some 32 publications. 30 The Bayle, Folkestone, Kent.

HURT, Freda Mary Elizabeth. **FOREST HILL,** London, 1911. Author of "The Body at Bowman's Hollow", "Death by Request", "Sweet Death", "So Dark a Shadow", "Seven Years Secret", "Death in the Mist", "A Witch at the Funeral", etc. 298 Pickhurst Rise, West Wickham, Kent BR3 0AY. *8, 9.*

HYDE, H(arford) Montgomery, M.A.(Oxon.), D.Lit.(Belfast), F.R.S.L., F.R.Hist.S., M.R.I.A., Barrister-at-Law, Author. **BELFAST,** Northern Island, 14 August 1907. *M.P. for North Belfast (1950–1959); U.K. Delegate to the Consultative Assembly of the Council of Europe, Strasbourg (1952–1955); Professor of History, University of the Punjab, Lahore, Pakistan (1959–1962). Recipient of Macmillan Centenary Award, 1946 (for biography "Mexican Empire").* Publications

71

include: "The Rise of Castlereagh", "Judge Jeffreys", "The Trials of Oscar Wilde", "Carson", "The Trial of Sir Roger Casement", "Sir Patrick Hastings", "The Quiet Canadian", "Norman Birkett", "Cynthia", "The Story of Lamb House Rye", "Lord Reading", "Henry James At Home", "The Other Love", "Their Good Names", "Stalin", etc. Westwell House, Tenterden, Kent. *1, 7, 8, 9, 10, 14.*

INGRAMS, Doreen (Constance). **LONDON,** 24 January 1906. *Joint recipient (with husband) of Royal Geographical Society Founder's Medal, and Royal Central Asian Society Lawrence Medal.* Publications include: "Report on the Social and Economic Condition of the Aden Protectorate", "A Time in Arabia", "Palestine Papers, 1917–1922: Seeds of Conflict", etc. 3 Westfield House, Tenterden, Kent, *8, 10.*

INGRAMS, William Harold, C.M.G., O.B.E., Colonial Administrator (retired). **SHREWSBURY,** 3 February 1897. *Awarded Class IV Order of Brilliant Star, Zanzibar (1927); conjointly with wife, Lawrence Memorial Medal (1939), and Founder's Medal of Royal Geographical Society (1940); Burton Memorial Medal (1943).* Publications include: "Dialects of Zanzibar Sultanate", "Chronology and Genealogies of Zanzibar Rulers", "Guide to Swahili Examinations", "Zanzibar, Its History and People", "School History of Mauritius", "School Geography of Mauritius", "Report on the Social, Economic and Political Condition of the Hadhramaut", "Arabia and the Isles", "Seven Across the Sahara", "Hong Kong", "Uganda: a crisis of Nationhood", "The Yemen: Imams, Rulers and Revolutions", etc. Uphousden, near Ash-next-Sandwich, Canterbury, Kent. *1, 8.*

IRWIN, John (Conran), Art Historian. **MADRAS,** India, 5 August 1917. *Keeper, Oriental Department, Victoria and Albert Museum, London.* Publications include: "Jamini Roy: a biography", "Origins of Chintz", etc. Bellmans Green, Edenbridge, Kent. *1, 8, 9.*

ISIS *see* TORBETT, Harvey Douglas Louis.

IZZARD, Ralph William Burdick, O.B.E., M.A.(Cantab.), F.Z.S., Foreign Correspondent. **BILLERICAY,** Essex, 1910. Author of "The Hunt for the Burn", "The Innocent on Everest", "The Abominable Snowman Adventure" (translated into 89 languages), "Smelling the Breezes" (with Molly Izzard), etc. 7 Calverley Park, Tunbridge Wells, **Kent.** *8.*

72

JACOBS, T. C. H. *see* PENDOWER, Jacques.

JEFFRIES, Graham Montague, Novelist. **LONDON,** 1900. (*pseud.* Bruce Graeme.) Author of More than 100 books since 1925, including: "The Story of Buckingham Palace", "The Story of St. James's Palace", "A Century of Buckingham Palace", "The Story of Windsor Castle", etc. Gorse Field Cottage, Aldington Frith, near Ashford, Kent. *1, 8, 9.*

JEFFRIES, Roderic (Graeme), Barrister-at-Law and Author. **LONDON,** 21 October 1926. (*pseud.* Roderic Graeme, Jeffrey Ashford.) Bourne Farm, Aldington Frith, near Ashford, Kent. *8, 9, 10.*

JEZARD, Alison, Teacher of English. **MAYFIELD,** Sussex, 7 September 1919. Garden Flat, 57 Earl's Avenue, Folkestone, Kent.

JOINER, C. L., M.D., F.R.C.P., Physician. **LONDON,** 1923. Author of "A Short Textbook of Medicine", etc. Ashton, Mead Road, Chislehurst, Kent. *8.*

JONES, Brian, B.A.(Cantab.), Teacher of English at Kent College, Canterbury. **LONDON,** 1938. Publications include: "Poems", "A Family Album", "Interior", etc. 106 St. Stephens Road, Canterbury, Kent. *8, 9, 12.*

KEEPING, Charles, N.D.D., M.S.I.A., Visiting Lecturer in Art. **LONDON,** 1924. Publications include: "Black Dolly", "Shaun and the Carthorse", "Charley, Charlotte and the Golden Canary", "Alfie and the Ferryboat", "Tinker Tailor", "Joseph's Yard", "Through the Window", etc. 16 Church Road, Shortlands, Bromley, Kent BR2 0HP. *8.*

KEITH-LUCAS, Bryan, M.A.(Cantab.), M.A.(Oxon.), Professor of Government, University of Kent at Canterbury, and Master of Darwin College. **FEN DITTON,** Cambridge, 1 August 1912. *Chairman, Electoral Reform Commission in Sierra Leone and Mauritius, 1954 and 1955; Chairman, National Association of Parish Councils, 1965– 1971; President, Kent Association of Parish Councils, since 1971.* Publications include: "Cripps on Compulsory Acquisition of Land" (with M. A. L. Cripps), "The English Local Government Franchise", "The History of Local Government in England", etc. Darwin College, The University, Canterbury, Kent. *1, 8.*

KELLY, Lady (Marie Noele), Travel Writer. **BRUSSELS,** Belgium. Author of "Mirror to Russia", "Turkish Delights", "Picture Book of Russia", "This Delicious Land, Portugal Dawn to Dusk", etc. Romden Castle, Smarden, Kent. *8, 9.*

KENRICK, Tony, Advertising Copywriter. **SYDNEY,** N.S.W. Australia, 1935. Author of "The only good body's a dead one". 25 Bromley Common, Bromley, Kent. *8.*

KING, W(illiam) Gordon, B.Sc.(Econ.)(London), B.Com.(Hons.) (London), Assistant Master, Dover Grammar School for Boys. **BATTLE,** Sussex, 29 June 1909. Author of "Livelihood of Man" (with H. M. Croome), Bushy Ruff, Goodwin Road, St. Margarets Bay, Dover, Kent.

KINGSBURY, Phyllis (May), Educational Writer. **HALIFAX,** Yorkshire. (*pseud.* Phyllis Flowerdew.) *Recipient of Diploma in the Psychology of Childhood (Birmingham University),* etc. Publications include: Flamingo Books, More Stories for Telling, Poetry is All Around, New Interest Books, etc. Fallows, 14 Chartway, Sevenoaks, Kent. *9, 14.*

KINKEAD-WEEKES, Mark, M.A.(Oxon.), Senior Lecturer, University of Kent at Canterbury. **PRETORIA,** Transvaal, Republic of South Africa, 1931. Publications include: "William Golding". South Mystole House, Mystole Park, Chartham, Kent. *8.*

KLAPPER, Charles Frederick, M.Inst.T., Editor. **BROMLEY-BY-BOW,** London, 1905. *Chairman, Metropolitan Section, Institute of Transport, 1957–1959; Sometime President, Railway and Canal Historical Society; President, The Omnibus Society, 1950; Chairman, Transport Tutorial Association.* Publications include: "Road Transport", "Modern Railway Operation" (3rd edition, with David R. Lamb), "Buses and Trams Annual", "The Golden Age of Tramways", etc. 45 Crest Road, Hayes, Bromley, Kent BR2 7JA. *8.*

KORNITZER, Margaret H(ester), Author and Journalist. **MONKS-EATON,** Northumberland. Author of "Modern Woman and Herself", "Child Adoption in the Modern World", "Adoption", "Mr. Fairweather and His Family", "Adoption and Family Life", etc. 107 Farnaby Road, Bromley, Kent BR1 4BN. *8.*

KORTH, Leslie O(swald), M.B.H.A.(Hon.), Psychotherapist. **SWAN-SEA,** Glamorgan, Wales, 23 July 1887. *Hon. Fellow and Life Member of the Acupuncture Association.* Wenvoe, 159 St. John's Road, Tunbridge Wells, Kent. *8, 9, 62.*

LORRAINE, Anne *see* CHISHOLM, Lilian.

LOVELL, John, B.A., Ph.D., University Lecturer. **BATH,** Somerset, 1940. Author of "A Short History of the T.U.C." (with B. C. Roberts), "Stevedores and Dockers", etc. Eliot College, The University, Canterbury, Kent. *8, 79.*

LOWE, C. W., B.Sc.(Hons.)(Aberystwyth), F.S.S. **ABERFAN,** Glamorgan, Wales, 1918. Author of "Critical Path Analysis by Bar Chart", "Industrial Statistics" (vols. 1 and 2), etc. 25 Ribston Close, Bromley, Kent BR2 8LS. *8, 62.*

LUBBOCK, Mary Katherine Adelaide (The Hon. Mrs. Mary Lubbock), Historian, Autobiographer and Travel Writer. High Elms House, Downe, Orpington, Kent. *9.*

LUSON, Pamela *see* BLAXLAND, Pamela C(live) M(ary).

McCONNELL, Jean, Writer and Playwright. **LONDON,** 18 November 1926. *Committee Member, Crime Writers' Association; Committee Member, Writers' Guild of Great Britain.* Publications include: "Haul for the Shore", "Pick of the Season", "Look out for the Catch", "The Red Cloak", "Wine in a Venetian Goblet", "Money's No Object", "It's a Gift", "One Man Band", "Blush Pink", "Chord on the Triangle", "Drama in the Making", "Blood on My Mind", etc. 9 Hadlow Road, Tonbridge, Kent. *8.*

McCORMICK, (George) Donald (King), Journalist. **RHYL,** Flintshire, Wales, 9 December 1911. (*pseud.* Richard Deacon.) Publications (under Donald McCormick): "Mask of Merlin", "Pedlar of Death", "The Identity of Jack the Ripper", "The Mystery of Lord Kitchener's Death", etc. Publications (under Richard Deacon); "Madoc and the Discovery of America", "A History of the British Secret Service", etc. Flat 3, The Old House, 36 Southend Road, Beckenham, Kent. *8, 10, 62.*

MacDONALD, Rt. Hon. Malcolm (John), O.M., P.C., M.A.(Oxon.), Chancellor of the University of Durham. **LOSSIEMOUTH,** Morayshire, Scotland, 1901. *Recipient of numerous honorary doctorates, etc. President, Royal Commonwealth Society, since 1971.* Publications include: "Down North", "The Birds of Brewery Creek", "Borneo People", "Angkor", "Birds in my India Garden", "Birds in the Sun", "Treasure of Kenya", "People and Places", etc. Raspit Hill, Ivy Hatch, Sevenoaks, Kent.   *1, 8, 9, 63.*

McINTOSH, Kinn Hamilton, Crime Novelist. **HUDDERSFIELD,** Yorkshire, 20 June 1930. (*pseud.* Catherine Aird.) Publications include: "The Religious Body", "A Most Contagious Game", "Henrietta Who?", "The Complete Steel", "A Late Phoenix", etc. Invergordon, Sturry, near Canterbury, Kent.   *8, 10, 58.*

MACINTYRE, Captain Donald, D.S.O., D.S.C., R.N. (retired). **DEHRA DUN,** India, 1904. Author of "U-Boat Killer", "Thunder of the Guns", "The Kola Run" (in collaboration with Vice Admiral Sir Ian Campbell), "Jutland", "Narvik", "Fighting Admiral", "The Battle of the Atlantic", "Battle for the Mediterranean", "Battle for the Pacific", "Admiral Rodney", etc. Sizergh, Little Chart, Ashford, Kent.   *8.*

McLELLAN, David, M.A.(Oxon), D.Phil.(Oxon.), University Teacher. **HERTFORD,** 10 February 1940. Author of "The Young Hegelians and Karl Marx", "Marx before Marxism", "The Thought of Karl Marx", etc. 122 Old Dover Road, Canterbury, Kent.   *8, 10.*

MAHOOD, Molly (Maureen), Professor of English Literature, Literary Critic. Rutherford College, University of Kent, Canterbury, Kent.   *9.*

MALET, Hugh *see* GRENVILLE-MALET, Baldwyn Hugh.

MANSFIELD, W(alter) K(enneth), B.Sc., Ph.D.(London), M.I.E.E., F.Inst.P., University Lecturer. **HORNSEY,** Middlesex, 20 October 1921. Author of "Elementary Nuclear Physics", "Reactor Physics" (translation), etc. 16 Hurstwood Drive, Bromley, Kent BR1 2JF.   *8.*

MARTIN, Charles Robert (or Rupert) Arthur, M.B., B.S.(London), L.R.C.P., M.R.C.S., D.P.H., D.P.A., F.R.S.H., LL.B., Barrister-at-Law. Medical Officer. **HIGH WYCOMBE,** Buckinghamshire, 25 May 1900. Publications include: "Practical Food Inspection", "Slums and Slummers", "Law Relating to Medical Practice", etc. Dean Garden, Fitzroy Road, Tankerton, Kent.   *8.*

MATHER, L(eonard) C(harles), B.Com.(London), F.I.B., F.C.I.S., Banker. **PORT SUNLIGHT,** Cheshire, 10 October 1909. Author of books on banking. Rochester House, Parkfield, Seal, Sevenoaks, Kent. *1, 2, 7, 9, 66.*

MAXWELL, Vicky *see* WORBOYS, Annette Isobel.

MEATES, Lieut.-Col. Geoffrey Wells, F.S.A. **HEREFORD,** 1900. *Chairman of Council, Kent Archaeological Society; Member of Council, Society of Antiquaries, 1956–1957; Director of Excavations, Lullingstone Roman Villa (from 1949); Founder of Darent Valley Research Group, 1947.* Publications include: "Lullingstone Roman Villa", etc. The Gate House, Lullingstone Castle, Eynsford, Kent. *8.*

MEDLYCOTT, Anthony, F.R.I.B.A., A.R.C.M., A.R.C.O., Lecturer. **CRANBORNE,** Dorset, 1909. Downe Hall, near Farnborough, Kent. *8, 79.*

MILLAR, Rev. Lynn Hartley, M.A., B.D., Ph.D., Clergyman. Author of "Christian Education in the First Four Centuries", "Problems of Christian Education". 38 Sidney Road, Gillingham, Kent.   *15.*

MILNE-THOMSON, L(ouis) M(elville), C.B.E., M.A.(Cantab.), Hon. Ph.D., Hon.Sc.D., F.R.S.E., Mathematician. **LONDON,** 1 May 1891. 2 Bullfinch Lane, Riverhead, Sevenoaks, Kent.   *1, 8.*

MINCHIN, Rev. Basil (George) (Francis), B.Sc.(Bristol), Clerk in Holy Orders. **GLOUCESTER,** 30 March 1910. Publications include: "Covenant and Sacrifice", "Every Man in his Ministry", "Outward and Visible", etc. Lynsted Vicarage, Sittingbourne, Kent.   *15.*

MINGAY, G(ordon) E(dmund), B.A.(Hons.), Ph.D., F.R.Hist.S., Professor of Agrarian History, University of Kent at Canterbury. **LONG EATON,** Derbyshire, 20 June 1923. Publications include: "English Landed Society in the Eighteenth Century", "The Agricultural Revolution 1750–1880" (with J. D. Chambers), "Land, Labour and Population in the Industrial Revolution" (edited, with E. L. Jones), "Britain and America" (with Philip S. Bagwell), etc. Rutherford College, University of Kent, Canterbury, Kent.   *8, 9.*

MOHAN, Talbot Greaves, M.A., Clergyman. **TORQUAY,** Devon, 29 August 1895. Author of "Your Bereavement". 18 Uplands Way, Sevenoaks, Kent.   *8, 9, 15, 79.*

77

MONK, Kathleen Doris, A.R.C.A., Senior Lecturer, Avery Hill College of Education. **LOWER KINGSWOOD,** Tadworth, Surrey, 1927. Author of "Fun with Fabric Printing". 5 Sutcliffe Road, Welling, Kent. *8.*

MOORE, Katharine, M.A.(Oxon.), Lecturer in English Literature. **HAMPSTEAD,** London, 1898. Publications include: "Moog", "A Treasury of the Kingdom" (in collaboration), "The Spirit of Tolerance", "Cordial Relations", "Kipling and the White Man's Burden", "Family Fortunes", "Women", etc. Riverside House, Shoreham, Sevenoaks, Kent. *8.*

MORGAN, Helen, Writer. **ILFORD,** Essex, 11 April 1921. Publications include: "The Little Old Lady", "Meet Mary Kate", "Tales of Tigg's Farm", "A Dream of Dragons", "Satchkin Patchkin", "Mary Kate and the Jumble Bear", "Mrs. Pinny and the Blowing Day", "Mrs. Pinny and the Sudden Snow", "Mary Kate and the School Bus", "Mother Farthing's Luck", "Two in the Garden", "Two in the House", "Two on the Farm", "Two by the Sea", "The Tailor and the Sailor and the Small Black Cat", "A Mouthful of Magic", "Mrs. Pinny and the Salty Sea Day", etc. Forcett House, Angley Road, Cranbrook, Kent. *8, 9.*

MOSS, John, C.B.E., Barrister-at-Law. **LOUGHBOROUGH,** Leicestershire, 12 June 1890. *Chairman, National Old People's Welfare Council, 1951–1967.* Author of several works on local government law and practice. Editor of "Local Government Law and Legislation", etc. 20 Cordova Court, Folkestone, Kent. *1, 8, 9.*

MOSS, Robert. **NUNEATON,** Warwickshire, 1903. Author of "The Golden Bar and Golden Ladder", "Strange Quest at Cliff House", "The Cliff House Monster", "Mystery at Gull's Nest", "Shy Girl at Southdown", etc. 110 Cumberland Road, Shortlands, Bromley, Kent. *8.*

MOULE, Rev. Arthur William Handley, M.A., Clergyman. Editor of of H. C. G. Moule's "Second Epistle of Paul to the Corinthians". Mabledon, Tonbridge, Kent. *15.*

MOYSE-BARTLETT, Hubert, M.B.E., M.A.(Oxon.), Ph.D.(London), Army Officer; University Administrator (retired). **SHRAWLEY,** Worcestershire, 12 February 1902. Author of "History of the Merchant Navy", "Great Movements in European History", "The King's African Rifles", "The Pirates of Trucial Oman", "Louis Edward Nolan and his Influence on the British Cavalry". 12 Marlborough Court, Earl's Avenue, Folkestone, Kent.

MURRAY, Joan, Former Teacher of Dancing. **NAINI TAL,** India, 4 June 1904. (*pseud.* Joan Wildeblood.) Author of "Apologie de la Danse", "The Polite World" (with P. Brinson). Technical editor of "Dances of Argentina", "Dances of Mexico". Tickners East, Hawkhurst, Kent. *8.*

NAIRNE, Charles John Campbell, B.A., Editor. **PERTH,** Scotland, 1909. Editor of "Parish Council's Review", etc. Author of "The Trossachs and the Rob Roy Country", "One Stair Up", "Stony Ground", "The Little Valley of God" (trans.), "The Secret Holiday" (trans.), etc. Tanglewood Cottage, Brittains Lane, Sevenoaks, Kent. *8, 9, 63.*

NEWPORT, Oliver William, F.R.G.S., F.R.P.S.,L., Editor and Journalist. **LONDON,** 8 December 1922. Author of "Channel Islands Stamps and Postal History", etc. Farm Cottage, 33 Halfway Street, Sidcup, Kent. *8, 9.*

NICOLSON, Nigel, M.B.E., M.A.(Oxon.), F.S.A., Author and Publisher. **LONDON,** 19 January 1917. *Sometime Member of Parliament.* Publications include: "People and Parliament", "Lord of the Isles", "Great Houses of Britain", "Great House", "Letters and Diaries of Harold Nicolson" (editor, 3 volumes), "Alex." (biography of Field Marshal Lord Alexander of Tunis), etc. Sissinghurst Castle, Kent. *1, 6.*

NIVEN, Sir (Cecil) Rex, Kt., C.M.G., M.C., M.A.(Hons.)(Oxon.), F.R.G.S., **OTARU,** Japan, 20 November 1898. Publications include: "A Short History of Nigeria", "Nigeria's Story", "Nigeria: the Outline of a Colony", "How Nigeria is Governed", "West Africa", "Short History of the Yoruba Peoples", "You and Your Government", "Nine Great Africans", "Nigeria", "My Life, by the late Sardauna of Sokoto" (in collaboration), "The War of Nigerian Unity", etc. The Old Cottage, Hope Road, Deal, Kent. *1, 8, 32.*

NORRIS, James Alfred, B.A.(Cantab.), Member BBC Secretariat. **LONDON,** 1929. Author of "The First Afghan War 1838–1842", etc. Devon Cottage, Bessels Green, Sevenoaks, Kent.   *8.*

NUNN, Ray, Journalist. **GREENWICH,** London, 1922. Author of "The Bumper Book of Sex", "You don't have to grow Old", etc. 104 West Common Road, Hayes, Bromley, Kent.   *8.*

NUTTER, Jack Crossley, M.A.(Cantab.), A.M.I.E.E., Company Director. **ROCHDALE,** Lancashire, 1925. Author of "Tridac—A Research Flight Simulator", "Power Station Instrumentation", "Analogue Computers in the Nuclear Power Programme", "An Electrical Process Control System for Nuclear Power Plant", etc. 38 Sutherland Avenue, Petts Wood, Kent.   *8, 35.*

OAKES, Philip, Journalist. **BURSLEM,** Staffordshire, 1928. Author of "Unlucky Joseph", "Exactly What We Want", "In the Affirmative", "The Godbrothers", etc. Pinnock Farm House Pluckley, Kent.   *8, 9, 66.*

OLDAKER, Rev. Wilfrid Horace, M.A.(Oxon.), Clergyman. Author of "Old Testament Prophecy" (parts 1–3), "Background of the Life of Jesus". Fir Tree Farm, Golford Road, Cranbrook, Kent.   *15.*

OSBORN, Rev. R(eginald) R(ichardson), M.A.(Oxon.), B.Litt.(Oxon.), Clergyman. **WIDNES,** Lancashire, 21 March 1912. Author of "Holy Communion in the Church of England", "Grounds of Hope" (editor and contributor), etc. St. Luke's Vicarage, 20 Bromley Common, Bromley, Kent BR2 9PD.   *15.*

OSBORNE, Margaret, L.R.A.M., L.R.C.M., Dog Breeder, Judge and Author. **WIMBLEDON PARK,** London, 12 October 1909. Author of "The Collie", "The Shetland Sheepdog", etc. Shiel, Stockbury, Sittingbourne, Kent.   *8, 9.*

PAINTER, Raymond, Freelance Financial Journalist. **LONDON,** 2 July 1934. Author of "Fortunes to be Made". 11 Matfield Close, Bromley, Kent BR2 9DY.

PAISLEY, Keith, A.M.I.Biol., A.M.I.E.T., Dip.Hort.(Wye), Lecturer in Soil Science. **WANSTEAD,** Essex, 1916. Author of "Dutch Lights", "Handbook of Organic Fertilisers", "Vegetable Growing in the Open", "Manures and Fertilizers", "Protected Cultivation", etc. Paddocks Farm, Stream Lane, Hawkhurst, Kent.   *8.*

PALMER, Rev. F(rancis) Noel, M.A.(Oxon.), B.D., Clergyman. **BEDFORD,** 13 December 1897. Author of "Christ's Way with People", "The Cross in History and Experience", "The Pattern of Life". 44 Princess Margaret Avenue, Cliftonville, Margate, Kent. *15.*

PALMER, Commander Joseph Mansergh, R.N., Editorial Consultant. **ALVERSTOKE,** Hampshire, 1912. Editor of "Navy" (1964–1970). Publications include: "Sunda Passage", etc. River Hall Farm, Biddenden, Kent. *8, 9, 78.*

PARKER, Richard, Teacher. **STANMORE,** Middlesex, 15 February 1915. Author of "The Old Powder Line", "Lion at Large", "Sword of Ganelon", etc. 36 Central Parade, Herne Bay, Kent.

PARKINSON, Frederick Charles Douglas, Art School Principal and Publisher. **ILFORD,** Essex, 1916. *Chairman, S. E. Federation of Art Societies, since 1950.* Author of "Type Identification Charts", etc. Bucksford Manor, Great Chart, Ashford, Kent. *8.*

PARRINDER, E(dward) G(eoffrey), M.A., D.D., Ph.D.(London), Professor of Comparative Study of Religions, University of London. **NEW BARNET,** Hertfordshire, 30 April 1910. *Wilde Lecturer in Natural and Comparative Religion, University of Oxford (1966– 1969); Charles Strong Memorial Lecturer, Australia (1964).* Publications include: "West African Religion", "Religion in an African City", "Witchcraft", "Comparative Religion", "World's Living Religions", "Jesus in the Quran", "African Mythology", "Religion in Africa", "Avatar & Incarnation", "Dictionary of Non-Christian Religions", etc. 31 Charterhouse Road, Orpington, Kent. *1, 8, 64.*

PEAR, T(om) H(atherley), M.A.(Manchester), B.Sc.(London), Emeritus Professor of Psychology, University of Manchester. **WALPOLE ST. PETER,** Norfolk, 22 March 1886. (*pseud.* Peter Hatherley.) *Sometime President, British Psychological Society, also former President, Psychology Section British Association.* Publications include: "Remembering and Forgetting", "Voice and Personality", "English Social Differences", "Personality, Appearance and Speech", "The Moulding of Modern Man", etc. Shirk Oak House, Woodchurch, Ashford, Kent. *1, 7, 8, 9.*

PENDOWER, Jacques, Author. **PLYMOUTH,** Devon, 30 December 1899. (*pseuds.* T. C. H. Jacobs, Penn Dower, Tom Curtis.) *Founder, Treasurer and Chairman (as T. C. H. Jacobs), Crime Writers' Association (1960–1961).* Author of more than 150 novels and several non-fiction works, etc. 44 Hill Crescent, Bexley, Kent.   *8, 9, 10, 79.*

PENN, William Samuel, B.Sc.(London), Chemist. **WOLVERHAMP-TON,** Staffordshire, 1922. Author of "High Polymeric Chemistry", "The Synthetic Rubber Technology", "P.V.C. Technology", etc. 27 Dobson Road, Gravesend, Kent.   *8, 66.*

PETERS, Ken, Magazine Editor. Writer on tape recording, etc. 4a Kings Road, Biggin Hill, Kent.   *9.*

POOLE, Rev. Stanley Burke-Roche, M.A.(London), Clergyman. Author of "Royal Mysteries and Pretenders". Littlebourne Vicarage, Canterbury, Kent.   *15.*

POSTER, Cyril Dennis, Headmaster. Writer on education. Parsonage Farm House, Parsonage Chase, Minster-in-Sheppey, Kent.   *9.*

POSTGATE, Raymond William, Author. **CAMBRIDGE,** 1896. Publications include: "Revolution from 1789 and 1906", "The Common People 1746–1946" (with G. D. H. Cole), "The Story of a Year, 1848", "That Devil Wilkes", "Life of George Lansbury", "The Good Food Guide", "The Plain Man's Guide to Wine", "A.B.C. of Choosing Wine", "H. G. Wells' Outline of History", "Verdict of Twelve", "Somebody at the Door", "The Ledger is Kept", "Every Man is God", "Story of a Year, 1798", "Portuguese Wines", etc. Red Lion Cottage, Blean, near Whitstable, Kent.   *8, 9.*

PRIOR, Rev. K(enneth) F(rancis) W(illiam), B.A., L.Th.(Durham), Clergyman. **LONDON,** 15 October 1926. Author of "God and Mammon", "The Way of Holiness". The Rectory, Sevenoaks, Kent. *8, 9, 14, 15.*

PUGH, John Charles, M.A.(Cantab.), Ph.D.(London), F.R.I.C.S., Professor of Geography. **BRISTOL,** Gloucestershire, 1919. Publications include: "Land and People in Nigeria" (with K. M. Buchanan), "A Short Geography of West Africa" (with A. E. Perry), "West Africa" (with W. B. Morgan), etc. 4 Connaught Way, Tunbridge Wells, Kent.   *8, 9.*

PYM, Christopher, Archaeologist. 132 Bromley Road, Beckenham, Kent. *9.*

RAINER, Dachine, M.A., Poet, Essayist and Fiction Writer. **NEW YORK,** U.S.A., 1921. Publications include: "Outside Time" (poems), "Prison Etiquette" (co-editor), "The Uncomfortable Inn", "'61 England", etc. Dwelly Farm, Edenbridge, Kent. *8, 9.*

RAMCHAND, Kenneth, M.A.(Hons.)(Edinburgh), Ph.D., University Lecturer. **TRINIDAD,** 1939. Author of "West Indian Narrative", "The West Indian Novel and Its Background", etc. Faculty of Humanities, University of Kent, Canterbury, Kent. *8.*

RAMSEY, Most Rev. and Rt. Hon. (Arthur) Michael, P.C., M.A., B.D., Hon.D.D., Hon. D.C.L., Hon.D.Litt., Archbishop of Canterbury. **CAMBRIDGE,** 14 November 1904. *President, English Association, 1958; President of the (Edinburgh) Sir Walter Scott Club, 1961.* Publications include: "The Gospel and the Catholic Church", "The Resurrection of Christ", "The Glory of God and the Transfiguration of Christ", "F. D. Maurice and the Conflicts of Modern Theology", "Durham Essays and Addresses", "From Gore to Temple", "Introducing the Christian Faith", "Canterbury Essays and Addresses", "Sacred and Secular", "God, Christ and the World", "The Future of the Christian Church" (with Cardinal Svenens), etc. Old Palace, Canterbury, Kent. *1, 6, 8, 15.*

RAY, Cyril, Writer. **MANCHESTER,** Lancashire, 16 March 1908. *Awarded Cavaliere dell'Ordine al Merito di Repubblica Italiana, 1972; Wine and Food Society's André Simon Prize, 1964. Founder, First Chairman, and now Hon. President, Circle of Wine Writers.* Publications include: "Scenes and Characters from Surtees", "From Algiers to Austria", "The History of 78th Division", "The Pageant of London", "Merry England", "Regiment of the Line: The Story of the Lancashire Fusiliers", "The Gourmet's Companion" (edited), "Morton Shand's Book of French Wines" (edited)), "Best Murder Stories" (edited), "The Wines of Italy", "In a Glass Lightly", "Lafite", "Bollinger"; also Editor, "The Compleat Imbiber" (Nos. 1–12, 1956–1971). Delmonden Manor, Hawkhurst, Kent. *1, 8, 9, 10, 35.*

G   83

RAY, John Philip, Dip.Hist., Senior Master, The Hugh Christie School, Tonbridge. **LONDON,** 5 May 1929. Publications include: "History of the Motor Car", "History of Britain, 1900–1939", "A History of Flight", "Britain and the Modern World", "The Victorian Age", "A History of Britain's Modern Transport", "History of the Railways", "Hitler and Mussolini", "Lloyd George and Churchill", "Roosevelt and Kennedy", "The Place of Women", "Schools since 1700", etc. Cherrytrees, Exeter Close, Tonbridge, Kent. *8, 9, 10.*

READ, Donald, B.Litt., M.A.(Oxon.), Ph.D.(Sheffield), F.R.Hist.S., Reader in Modern History, University of Kent. Born 31 July 1930. *Chairman, Local History Committee, Historical Association.* Author of "Peterloo", "Press and People, 1790–1850", "The English Provinces, 1760–1960", "Cobden and Bright", "Feargus O'Conner" (with Eric Glasgow), "Edwardian England, 1901–1915", etc. Darwin College, University of Kent at Canterbury, Canterbury, Kent. *7, 9.*

REES, Jean Anglin. **NEWCASTLE UPON TYNE,** Northumberland, 1912. Author of "Lady with Sun Lamp", "Wedding Present", "Stranger Than Fiction", "Fire in his Bones", "Road to Sodom", "Jacob Have I Loved", "Danger! Devils at Work", "God Wondered", "Back to Balcomrie", etc. Hildenborough Hall, Otford Hills, Sevenoaks, Kent. *8.*

REEVE-JONES, Alan Edmond, Writer and Television Commentator, etc. **BERGEN,** Norway, 1914. Author of "London Pubs", etc. Walnut Tree Cottage, Herne Common, near Canterbury, Kent. *8.*

REID, Gavin Hunter, B.A.(London), Clergyman. **GREENOCK,** Renfrewshire, Scotland, 1934. *Publications Secretary, Church Pastoral Aid Society, since 1966.* Author of "The Gagging of God", etc. Fireflies, Leesons Hill, Chislehurst, Kent. *8, 63.*

REYNOLDS, Christopher, A.R.C.A., Biology Teacher. **BRINSCALL,** Lancashire, 1911. Author of "Small Creatures in my Back Garden", "The Pond on my Window-Sill", etc. 40 Fitzroy Avenue, Kingsgate, Broadstairs, Kent. *8.*

RICHARDSON, R(obert) G(alloway), M.A., B.M., B.Ch.(Oxon.), Consultant Medical Editor (Registered Medical Practitioner). **LONDON,** 2 October 1926. Author of "The Surgeon's Tale—A History of Modern Surgery", "Surgery: Old and New Frontiers", "The Surgeon's Heart—A History of Cardiac Surgery", etc. The Old Cottage, 258 Bromley Road, Shortlands, Kent. *8, 9.*

RITCHIE, Carson Irvine Alexander, Lecturer in History, Woolwich Polytechnic, London. Writer of instructional manuals on sculpture; also historian and writer of short stories. The Carmont, 4 Hurst Place, Stanham Road, Dartford, Kent. *9.*

ROBERTSON, Helen *see* EDMISTON, (Helen) Jean (Mary).

ROBINSON, Godfrey Clive, B.A.(London), B.D., Baptist Minister. **MURREE HILLS,** India, 1913. Author of "The Way" (in collaboration), "The King's Business", "Here is the Answer", "Colony of Heaven", "The Art of Living", "Companions of the Way", "Our Returning King", "The Christian's Conduct", etc. 32 Wendover Road, Bromley, Kent. *8, 9.*

RODGERS, Betsy (Lady Rodgers), M.A., Ph.D., J.P. **PAIGNTON,** Devon. Author of "Comedy in Germany in the Eighteenth Century", "Cloak of Charity", "Georgian Chronicle", "Mrs. Barbauld and her Family", etc. The Dower House, Groombridge, Kent. *8, 9, 79.*

RODGERS, Sir John (Charles), Bart., M.A.(Hons.) (Oxon.), F.R.S.A., M.P., Author, Broadcaster, Company Director. **YORK,** 5 October 1906. *Knight Grand Cross, Order of Civil Merit (Spain); Grand Cross of Liechtenstein; Commander, Order of Don Henrique (Portugal). For several years a Member of the Executive Council of The Society of Authors, etc.* Publications include: "The Old Public Schools of England", "The English Woodland", "English Rivers", "York", "Poems of Thomas Gray" (edited), "Mary Ward Settlement: a History", etc. The Dower House, Groombridge, Kent. *1, 6, 7, 8, 58.*

RODNEY, Bob *see* RODRIGO, Robert.

RODRIGO, Robert, Journalist. **NEWMARKET,** Suffolk, 11 April 1928. (*pseud.* Bob Rodney.) Publications include: "The Racing Game", "Search and Rescue", "Peter May", "The Braddocks" (with Bessie and Jack Braddock), "Master Golfer" (with Jimmy Hitchcock), "The Birdie Book", "The Paddock Book", "Golf with Gregson" (with Malcolm Gregson), "I Paid the Piper" (with John Joel), etc. 14 Oaklands Road, Groombridge, Kent. *9.*

ROE, Rev. James Moulton, M.A., Clergyman. Author of "A History of the British and Foreign Bible Society, 1905–1954". The Vicarage, 51 Hayes Road, Bromley, Kent BR2 9AE. *15.*

RUSH, Philip, Writer. **PALMERS GREEN,** London 24 February 1908. Author of "Rogue's Lute", "Mary Read, Buccaneer", "Freedom Is The Man", "Crispin's Apprentice", "A Cage of Falcons", "Apprentice-at-Arms", "Strange People", "More Strange People", "Strange Stuarts", "Great Men of Sussex", "The Castle and the Harp", "Frost Fair", "That Fool of a Priest", etc. 45 Castle Street, Canterbury, Kent.   *7, 8.*

RYAN, Isobel Laura. **CABRI,** Saskatchewan, Canada, 1918. Author of "Black Man's Country", "Black Man's Town", "Black Man's Palaver", "The Crane", etc. 47 Lower Green Road, Pembury, Tunbridge Wells, Kent.   *8.*

SACKVILLE, Lady *see* HICHENS, Jacobine Napier.

SAVIDGE, Alan (W. J.), M.A.(London), Assistant Secretary to the Church Commissioners (retired). **LONDON,** 11 June 1903. Publications include: "The Foundation and Early Years of Queen Anne's Bounty", "The Parsonage in England: Its History and Architecture". 2 Oak Tree Close, Rodmell Road, Tunbridge Wells, Kent.

SCORPIO *see* TUCKER, W(illiam) J(oseph).

SELLERS, Leslie, Production Editor, "Daily Mail". Writer of non-fiction. Cedar House, Pines Road, Bromley, Kent BR1 2AA.   *9.*

SERJEANT, Richard *see* VAN ESSEN, William.

SEYMOUR, Henry *see* HARTMANN, Henry.

SEYMOUR, Paul, M.Sc.(London), F.R.E.S., Biologist. 70 Prospect Road, Tunbridge Wells, Kent.

SHAH, Idries, F.R.S.A., F.R.Econ.S., Author. **SIMLA,** India, 16 June 1924. Publications include: "Oriental Magic", "Destination Mecca", "The Sufis", "Special Problems", "Exploits of the Incomparable Mulla Nasrudin", "Tales of the Dervishes", "Secret Lore", "Pleasantries of the Incredible Mulla Nasrudin", "Reflections", "The Way of The Sufi", "Wisdom of the Idiots", "The Book of The Book", "The Dermis Probe", "Thinkers of The East", "The Magic Monastery", etc. c/o Jonathan Cape Limited, Publishers, 30 Bedford Square, London WC1B 3EL. *Resident in Kent.*   *8, 9, 10, 11, 14, 45, 50, 56, 70.*

SHARP, Doreen Maud, F.R.S.A., F.S.C.T., F.F.T.Com., Senior Lecturer in Commercial Subjects, Bromley College of Technology. **UPPER NORWOOD,** London, 21 February 1920. *Moderator and Examiner, Royal Society of Arts and London Chamber of Commerce.* Co-author, with H. M. Crozier, of "Secretarial Typing", "Secretarial Dictation", "Teachers' Handbook and Solutions", "Through Practice to Production", "Mailable Copy", etc. 4 Seabrook Drive, West Wickham, Kent. *8, 9.*

SILLITOE, Alan, Writer. **NOTTINGHAM,** 4 March 1928. *Awarded Hawthornden Prize for Literature, 1960.* Publications include: "Saturday Night and Sunday Morning", "The Loneliness of the Long Distance Runner", "Key to the Door", "The Ragman's Daughter", "The Death of William Posters", "A Tree on Fire", "Guzman Go Home", "All Citizens are Soldiers" (with Ruth Fainlight), "A Start in Life", "Travels in Nihilon", "Raw Material", etc. Wittersham, Kent. *1, 2, 6, 8, 9, 11, 12.*

SIMMONS, Catherine *see* DUNCAN, Kathleen Mary.

SIMMONS, Kim *see* DUNCAN, Kathleen Mary.

SIMS-WILLIAMS, Rev. Michael Vernon Sims, M.A.(Cantab.), Clergyman and Schoolmaster. **CHELSEA,** London, 1909. Author of "Camps for Men", "By Action and Debate", "Jeremy Prentice", "The Christian Apprenticeship of a Boy and his Friends", "Religion Through Drama", "The Christie Saga, History of S.P.G., 1701–1951", "Scripture in Class", BBC "Bible in Life" Series, "Using the Catechism", "Using the Revised Catechism", etc. Broumfield Borden, Sittingborne, Kent. *8, 15.*

SKRIBER, Orlando *see* SMITH, G(ordon) Roland.

SLOAN, P. *see* SLOAN, Patrick (Alan).

SLOAN, P. A. *see* SLOAN, Patrick (Alan).

SLOAN, Pat *see* SLOAN, Patrick (Alan).

SLOAN, Patrick (Alan), B.A.(Cantab.), Writer, Lecturer and Teacher. **GOSFORTH,** Newcastle upon Tyne, Northumberland, 19 May 1908. (Writes under: Pat Sloan, P. Sloan, P. A. Sloan.) Publications include: "Soviet Democracy", "Russia Without Illusions", "How the Soviet State is Run", "Russia Friend or Foe?", "Russia in Peace and War", "Russia Resists", "Guide to Economics", etc. 1 Bucks Cross Cottages, Chelsfield, Orpington, Kent. *8.*

SMAILES, Arthur Eltringham, M.A.(London), D.Lit., F.R.G.S., Professor of Geography. **HALTWHISTLE,** Northumberland, 23 March 1911. *President, Institute of British Geographers, 1970, and Hon. Secretary, 1951–1962.* Publications include: "The Geography of Towns", "North England", etc. 20 Marlborough Crescent, Sevenoaks, Kent. *1, 8.*

SMITH, G(ordon) Roland, L.S.I.A., A.C.P., Teacher, Artist, and Author. **WESTCLIFF-ON-SEA,** Essex, 6 March 1931. (*pseud.* Orlando Skriber.) *President, "Seminar Books", (New Church Missionary Society).* Publications include: "First Models in Cardboard", "Creative Crayon Craft", "Making a Model Village", "My Side of the Grave", "The Zebra Book of Papercraft", etc. Melilot, Well Hill Lane, Chelsfield, Orpington, Kent BR6 7QJ. *8.*

SMITH, Peter C(harles), Sales Office Manager. **NORTH ELMHAM,** Norfolk, 15 October 1940. Publications include: "Destroyer Leader", "Task Force 57", "Pedestal", "Stuka at War", "Hard Lying", "British Battlecruisers", etc. 25 Collet Walk, Park Wood, Rainham, Kent. *8.*

SPENCE, Canon Horace, M.A., B.Mus., Clergyman. Author of "An Anglican Use", "Decently and in Order", "Praises with Understanding". 2 South Close, The Precincts, Canterbury, Kent. *15.*

STACEY, (Leslie) Roy, Publisher. Editor of "Amateur Stage", etc. 1 Hawthorndene Road, Hayes, Bromley, Kent. *9.*

STANFIELD, Nancy Fisher, A.R.C.A., Art Teacher. **NUNEATON,** Warwickshire, 30 September 1905. Publications include: "Art for African Schools", "A Handbook of Art Teaching in Tropical Schools", etc. The Oasts, Great Comp, Borough Green, Kent. *8, 10.*

STANTON, Paul *see* BEATY, (Arthur) David.

STEVENS, James Hay, C.Eng., A.F.R.Ae.S., Editor. **LONDON,** 1913. Author of "The Shape of the Aeroplane", "Scale Model Aircraft", "The How and Why of Aircraft" (in collaboration), "An Introduction to the Auvergne", etc. Bottle Farm, Hart Hill, Charing, Ashford, Kent. *8, 9.*

STEWART, Norman, N.D.H., Head of Horticultural Department, Kent Farm Institute. **PAISLEY,** Renfrewshire, Scotland, 1914. *Chairman, Fruit Committee, Horticultural Educ. Association, 1954–1959.* Publications include: "Middleton's Gardening Guide", "Chrysanthemums", "Vegetables for Profit and Pleasure", "Better Pruning of Fruit", "Strawberries". Also author of other books in collaboration with Roy Hay and Edward Hyams. 4 Park Drive, Sittingbourne, Kent.   *8.*

STONER, C(harles) R(obert), B.Sc.(Eng.)(London), F.I.E.E., University Reader in Electrical Engineering (retired). **CROWBOROUGH,** Sussex, 22 October 1900. Author (with A. W. Ladner) of "Short Wave Wireless Communication". 216 Hayes Lane, Bromley, Kent. BR2 7LA.   *8, 29.*

SWANTON, Ernest William, O.B.E., Cricket and formerly Rugby Football Correspondent to the "Daily Telegraph". **LONDON,** 11 February 1907. *Editorial Director, "The Cricketer".* Publications include: "A History of Cricket" (with H. S. Altham), "Denis Compton, A Cricket Sketch", "Elusive Victory" (with F. R. Brown's Team in Australia), "Cricket and the Clock", "Best Cricket Stories" (An Anthology), "The Test Matches of 1953", "West Indian Adventure", "Victory in Australia, 1954–1955", "The Test Matches of 1956", "Report from South Africa" (with P. B. H. May's MCC Team, 1956–1957), "West Indies Revisited", "The Ashes in Suspense", "The World of Cricket" (General Editor), "Cricket from all Angles", etc. Delf House, Sandwich, Kent.   *1, 8.*

SYROP, Konrad, LL.B., General Programme Editor, BBC External Service. **VIENNA,** Austria, 1914. Author of "Spring in October", "The Polish Revolution of 1956", "Poland Between the Hammer and the Anvil", also various published translations. 10 Hayes Road, Bromley, Kent BR2 9AA.   *8, 9.*

TAPLIN, Walter, M.A.(Oxon.), B.Com.(London), Journalist. **SOUTHAMPTON,** Hampshire, 4 August 1910. Publications include: "Advertising: A New Approach", "Origin of Television Advertising", "History of the British Steel Industry" (with J. C. Carr), etc. Kent Hatch Lodge, Crockham Hill, near Edenbridge, Kent.   *1, 6, 7, 8, 9, 78.*

THOMAS, Denis, B.A.(Oxon.), Editor. **LONDON,** 1922. Author of "Personal Opinion", "Competition in Radio", "Copyright and the Creative Artist", "The Story of Newspapers", "Thomas Churchyard of Woodbridge", "The Mind of Economic Man", "The Visible Persuaders", "Concise Encyclopedia of Antiques", etc. Coach House, Oakwood Close, Chislehurst, Kent. *8.*

THRASHER, P(eter) A(dam), B.A., B.Sc.(Eng.), M.I.C.E., M.R.I.N.A., Chartered Civil Engineer. **PLYMOUTH,** Devon, 15 May 1923. Author of "Pasquale Paoli", etc. 1b Denbridge Road, Bickley, Bromley, Kent BR1 2AG. *8, 79.*

TOMPKINS, J(oyce) M(arjorie) S(anxter), D.Lit.(London), University Lecturer (retired). **CATFORD,** London, 1897. Publications include: "Popular Novel in England, 1700–1800", "The Polite Marriage", "The Art of Rudyard Kipling". White Cottage, The Common, Cranbrook, Kent. *8.*

TORBETT, Harvey Douglas Louis, Training Aids Adviser (Educational Technology). **SHEPHERDS BUSH,** London, 26 January 1921. (*pseud.* Isis.) Publications include: "Anglers Freshwater Fishes", "Coarse Fishing Museum", "Sea Fishing Museum". 9 Langley Road, Welling, Kent. *8, 9, 10.*

TREMAYNE, Sydney (Durward), Journalist and Poet. **AYR,** Scotland, 15 March 1912. *Scottish Arts Council Award, 1970.* Publications include: "Time and the Wind", "The Hardest Freedom", "The Rock and the Bird", "The Swans of Berwick", "The Turning Sky", "Selected and New Poems", etc. Blawan Orchard, Westerham Hill, Kent. *7, 8, 9, 12, 63.*

TREWMAN, Harry Frederick, M.A.(Cantab.), C.Eng., F.I.E.E., F.I.Mech.E., F.I.E.R.E., Managing Director (retired). **LONDON,** 1892. *Governor, Norwood Technical College.* Publications include: "Railway Electrification", "Mechanical Inspection", "Electronics as a Career", etc. High Pines, Marlings Park Avenue, Chislehurst, Kent. *8.*

TUCKER, A(rchibald) N(orman), M.A.(Cape Town), Ph.D.(London), D.Lit.(London), Emeritus Professor of East African Language. **CAPE TOWN**, South Africa, 10 March 1904. *Sometime member of Council, International African Institute.* Publications include: "Comparative phonetics of Suto-Chuana", "Primitive Tribal Music and Dancing in the Southern Sudan", "Disappointed Lion and other stories from the Bari of Central Africa", "The Eastern Sudanic Languages", "Swahili Phonetics" (with E. O. Ashton), "The Luganda Grammar" (in collaboration), "A Maasai Grammar" (in collaboration), "The Non-Bantu languages of N.E. Africa" (in collaboration), "Linguistic Analyses" (in collaboration), etc. 76 Granville Road, Sevenoaks, Kent. *1, 8, 9.*

TUCKER, Theodore F(rederic), O.B.E. **LONDON**, 19 February 1899. Publications include: "Sex Education in Schools", "Awkward Questions of Childhood", "Sex Problems and Youth", "Children Without Homes", etc. Bull's Hollow Cottage, Rusthall, Tunbridge Wells, Kent. *7, 8, 14.*

TUCKER, W(illiam) J(oseph), D.Sc., Ph.D., F.B.I.S., Science Researcher, Author and Publisher. **DALSTON**, London, 19 November 1896. (*pseud.* Scorpio.) Publications include: "The How of the Human Mind", "Your Stars of Destiny", "The How, What and Why of Astrology", "Principles of Scientific Astrology", "The Fixed Stars and Your Horoscope", "Scientific Prediction", "Astrology for Every-man", "Foundations of Astrology", "Astronomy for Students of Astrology", "Astrology and your Family Tree", "Harmony of the Spheres", "It is in the Stars", "Ptolemaic Astrology", "Astrology and the Abnormal Mind", "Physics and Astrology", "Autobiography of an Astrologer", "Predicting from the Stars", "Stars Over England", "Forecasting World Events", "Astromedical Diagnosis", "Astro-medical Research", "Investigating and Co-ordinating the Psyche", "Genetics and Astrology", etc. 45 Penshurst Avenue, Sidcup, Kent DA15 9EZ. *8, 24.*

TURING, John Ferrier, Solicitor. **COONOOR**, South India, 1908. Author of "Moving House", "Nothing Certain But Tax", "101 Points on Buying a House", "My Nephew Hamlet", etc. Flat C, 3 Hayne Road, Beckenham, Kent. *8.*

TURNOR, Christopher Reginald, M.A.(Oxon.), A.R.I.B.A. **HOVE,** Sussex, 1903. Author of "Polite Scene", "Bring Them Up Alive", "Pity the Guilty", "The Quiet Voice", "The Tiger and the Rose", "Nineteenth Century Architecture in Britain", "The Smaller English House", "James Wyatt", "The Spotted Dog", "Vision of England: Sussex, Oxfordshire, Kent", etc. Norman Street House, Ide Hill, Sevenoaks, Kent. *8.*

VAN ESSEN, William, F.R.C.S., Consultant Surgeon. **SNARESBROOK,** Essex, 26 July 1910. (*pseud.* Richard Serjeant.) Publications include: "Private Flying for Leisure and Business", "A Man May Drink", "The Spectrum of Pain", "Louis Pasteur and the Fight Against Disease", etc. 32 Oakhill Road, Beckenham, Kent.   *8.*

VINAVER, Eugene, M.A., D.Litt., D.ès L., Emeritus Professor. **ST. PETERSBURG,** Russia, 18 June 1899. *Recipient of numerous awards, including Chevalier of the Legion of Honour (France), honorary doctorates, etc.* Publications include: "The Love Potion in the Primitive Tristan Romance", "Malory", "Principles of Textual Emendation", "The Rise of Romance", "The Works of Sir Thomas Malory" (3 vols.), "Malory's Tale of the Death of King Arthur", "King Arthur and His Knights", etc. 27 Palace Street, Canterbury, Kent.   *1, 8, 9.*

WALSH, John Herbert, B.A.(London), Dip.Ed., Schoolmaster. **BRIGHTON,** Sussex, 1911. Publications include: "The Roundabout by the Sea and Other Verses for Children", "Teaching English", "The Truants and Other Poems for Children", "The House in the Cedar Tree", "Strawberry Town", etc. 26 Tudor Drive, Otford, Sevenoaks, Kent.   *8.*

WARREN, Charles Esmé Thornton, M.B.E., M.S.M. **PURLEY,** Surrey, 1912. Author of "Above Us the Waves", "The Admiralty Regrets", "Will Not We Fear", etc. Tile House, Bickley Park Road, Bickley, Kent.   *8.*

WATSON, James, B.A.(Hons.), Lecturer. **DARWEN,** Lancashire, 8 November 1936. Publications include: "Sign of the Swallow", "The Bull Leapers", etc. Flat B2, Vale Towers, 58 London Road, Tunbridge Wells, Kent.   *8, 9, 35.*

WEATHERALL, Miles, M.A., D.M., D.Sc.(Oxon.), F.I.Biol. M.P.S. (Hon.), Pharmacologist. **LONDON**, 14 October 1920. Publications include: "Statistics for Medical Students" (with L. Bernstein), "Scientific Method", etc. Wellcome Research Laboratories, Beckenham, Kent BR3 3BS. *1, 8.*

WEISS, Francis, Historian and Poet. 74 Overbury Avenue, Beckenham, Kent. *9.*

WELLS, Arthur Walter, Newspaper Editor-in-Chief (retired). **BOURNE**, Lincolnshire, 1894. Author of "All This Is Ended", "Southern Africa Today and Yesterday", "The Secret of a City", etc. 10 Castle Hill Court, 23 Castle Hill Avenue, Folkestone, Kent. *8.*

WELSBY, Canon Paul Antony, M.A., Ph.D., Clergyman. Author of Services and Prayers for Country Use", "A Modern Catechism", "Lancelot Andrewes, 1555–1626", "How the Church of England Works", "The Bond of Church and State", "George Abbot, the Unwanted Archbishop", etc. Southgate, The Precinct, Rochester, Kent. *15.*

WESTERN-HOLT, J. C. *see* HEMING, Commander Jack C(hetwynd) W(estern).

WHEELER, Terence, Lecturer in English, Christ Church College, Canterbury, Kent. Novelist. 6 West Cliff, Whitstable, Kent. *9.*

WHITE, Constance M., Author. **CROYDON**, London. Author of 45 books for children, including: "The Button Trail", "Suspect at St. Marks", etc. Flat 1, Woodlands, Park Road, Southborough, Tunbridge Wells, Kent. *8, 9.*

WHITE, Elizabeth Evelyne McIntosh, M.A., B.Sc. **SCOTLAND.** *Editor of "The Schoolmistress", 1927–1937.* Author of "Primary English", "Poetry for the Primary School", "Practical Modern English", "Russell Dramatic Readers", "Teach Yourself to Cook", "Come Cooking With Me", "Cook Without Fears", etc. Flat 2, 8 The Leas, Folkestone, Kent. *8, 63.*

WHITEHEAD, Lt.-Col. J(ohn) G(arway) O(utram), Army Officer (retired). **PEMBRIDGE**, Herefordshire, 27 February 1897. 10 Blackfriars Street, Canterbury, Kent. *8.*

WHITEHOUSE, Rev. W(alter) A(lexander), M.A.(Cantab. and Oxon.), B.Litt.(Oxon.), D.D.(Edinburgh), University Teacher of Theology. SHELLEY, near Huddersfield, Yorkshire, 27 February 1915. Author of "Christian Faith and the Scientific Attitude", "Biblical Doctrine of Justice and Law", "Order, Goodness, Glory", "Christian Confidence", etc. Eliot College, The University, Canterbury, Kent. *1, 8, 9, 58.*

WIGAN, Rev. Bernard John, M.A., Clergyman. Canon of Rochester Cathedral. Editor of "The Liturgy in English". Kingsdown, Somerfield Road, Maidstone, Kent. *9, 15.*

WILDEBLOOD, Joan *see* MURRAY, Joan.

WILLIAMSON, Catherine Ellis, Author, Lecturer and Traveller. CLARA, Offaly, Ireland, 1 May 1896. *First Woman Mayor of Canterbury (1938–1939, 1939–1940).* Publications include: "Though the Streets Burn", "The Crimson Dawn", "Come Along with Me". 2 Lady Woottons Green, Canterbury, Kent.

WILLIS, Lord (Edward Henry), F.R.S.A., Author. TOTTENHAM, London, 13 January 1918. *Recipient of Writers' Guild of Great Britain Award for Distinguished Service to Writing; Royal Society of Arts Silver Medal; Television Society Medal for Services to Television; Critics Award, Berlin Festival (1957). Past President, Writers' Guild of Great Britain; Executive Committee Member, League of Dramatists.* Publications include: "The Blue Lamp", "Woman in a Dressing Gown", "Whatever Happened to Tom Mix?", etc. 5 Shepherds Green, Chislehurst, Kent BR7 6PB. *1, 8, 9, 31, 32.*

WILLIS, Arthur J(ames), F.R.I.C.S., F.S.G., Chartered Quantity Surveyor and Genealogist. CONSTANTINOPLE, Turkey, 16 January 1895. Publications include: "Working Up a Bill of Quantities", "Some Notes on Taking Off Quantities", "To be a Surveyor", "An Example in Quantity Surveying", "Elements of Quantity Surveying" (in collab.), "More Advanced Quantity Surveying" (in collab.), "Practice and Procedure for the Quantity Surveyor" (in collab.), "Specification Writing for Architects and Surveyors" (in collab.), "The Architect in Practice" (in collab.), "Canterbury Marriage Licences 1751–1780", "Canterbury Marriage Licences 1781–1809", "Canterbury Marriage Licences 1810–1837", "Canterbury Licences (General) 1568–1646", "Hampshire Marriage Licences 1607–1640", "Hampshire Marriage

94

Licences 1669–1680", "Hampshire Marriage Allegations 1689–1837 (Supplement)", "Wills, Administrations and Inventories with the Winchester Diocesan Records", "Winchester Settlement Papers 1667–1842", "Winchester Guardianships after 1700", "Winchester Ordinations 1600–1829: I—Ordinands' Papers 1734–1827, II—Bishop's Registers, Subscription Books and Exhibition of Orders", "A Hampshire Miscellany", "Winchester Consistory Court Depositions", "A Calendar of Southampton Apprenticeship Registers 1609–1740" (in collab.), "Borough Sessions Papers 1653–1688" (Portsmouth Record Series, in collab.), "Genealogy for Beginners", "Introducing Genealogy," etc. Hambledon, Church Road, Lyminge, Folkestone, Kent. *8, 9, 10.*

WILLIS, Ted *see* WILLIS, Lord (Edward Henry).

WINCH, Michael B(luett), B.A.(Cantab.), Antique Exporter. **LONDON,** 6 December 1907. Publications include: "Republic for a Day", "Introducing Germany", "Introducing Belgium", "Austria", etc. Boughton-Monchelsea Place, near Maidstone, Kent. *8, 9, 10.*

WINKWORTH, D(erek) W(illiam), A.R.I.C.S., Quantity Surveyor. **FULHAM,** London, 11 March 1924. (*pseud.* 5029.) Author of "Railway Holiday in Portugal". 61 Rowan Walk, Bromley, Kent. *8.*

WOODFORDE, John (Edward) (Ffooks), B.A.(Hons.)(Cantab.), Writer. **LONDON,** 10 April 1925. Publications include: "Observer's Book of Furniture", "The Strange Story of False Teeth", "The Truth About Cottages", "The Story of the Bicycle", "The Strange Story of False Hair", "Furnishing a Country Cottage", etc. Worten House, Great Chart, Ashford, Kent. *8, 10.*

WORBOYS, Annette Isobel, Novelist and Short Story Writer. **AUCKLAND,** New Zealand. (*pseuds.* Annette Eyre, Vicky Maxwell.) Author of 17 romantic novels, including "The Magnolia Room", "The Little Millstones", "Rainbow Child", etc. The White House, Leigh, near Tonbridge, Kent. *8, 9.*

WORRALL, Ralph Lyndal, M.B., Ch.M., D.P.H., Medical Statistician. **SYDNEY,** N.S.W., Australia, 1903. Author of "The Outlook of Science", "Energy and Matter", "A Formula for Deriving Nuclear Power from Fusion Reactions at Very Low Temperatures", etc. 31 Braeside Avenue, Sevenoaks, Kent. *8.*

95

YOUNG, (Charles) Kenneth, B.A.(Leeds), F.R.S.L., Political and Literary Adviser to Beaverbrook Newspapers. **MIDDLESTOWN,** Wakefield, Yorkshire, 27 November 1916. *Editor of "The Yorkshire Post", 1960–1964; Governor, Welbeck College.* Author of "D. H. Lawrence", "John Dryden" (critical biography), "Ford Madox Ford", "The Bed Post" (edited), "The Second Bed Post" (edited), "A J. Balfour" (authorised biography), "Churchill and Beaverbrook: a Study in friendship and politics", "Rhodesia and Independence: A Study in British Colonial Policy", "Sir Compton Mackenzie, an Essay", "Music's Great Days in the Spas and Watering-places", "The Greek Passion: a study in people and politics", "Sir Alec Douglas-Home", etc. Amberfield, Chart Sutton, Kent.   *1, 6, 8, 9, 58.*

YOUNG, Edward Preston, D.S.O., D.S.C., Company Director and Publisher. **TRINIDAD,** British West Indies, 17 November 1913. Author of "One of Our Submarines", "Look at Lighthouses", "The Fifth Passenger", "Look at Submarines", etc. Horton Cottage, Monks Horton, Kent.   *1, 8.*

County Authors Today Series

Hon. General Editor: Geoffrey Handley-Taylor, Ph.D., F.R.S.L.

ALREADY PUBLISHED:

Lancashire Authors Today
Yorkshire Authors Today
Authors of Wales Today
Scottish Authors Today
Cheshire, Derbyshire and Staffordshire Authors Today
Berkshire, Hampshire and Wiltshire Authors Today
Devon, Dorset and Somerset Authors Today
Kent Authors Today
Sussex Authors Today

FORTHCOMING TITLES:

East Anglian Authors Today (Cambridgeshire, Essex, Norfolk Suffolk)
West Midlands Authors Today (Shropshire, Warwickshire, Worcestershire)
Northern Ireland Authors Today (The Six Counties)
East Midlands Authors Today (Leicestershire, Lincolnshire, Huntingdonshire, Northamptonshire, Nottinghamshire, Rutland)
Northern Authors Today (Cumberland, Durham, Northumberland, Westmorland)
Surrey Authors Today
Cornish Authors Today
Gloucestershire and Herefordshire Authors Today
Bedfordshire, Buckinghamshire, Hertfordshire and Oxfordshire Authors Today
London Authors Today (in four volumes).

Published by Eddison Press Ltd., 2 Greycoat Place
Westminster, London S.W.1